Conducting the Home Visit in Child Protection

Conducting the Home Visit in Child Protection

Second edition

Joanna Nicolas

Open University Press

Open University Press
McGraw-Hill Education
McGraw-Hill House
Shoppenhangers Road
Maidenhead
Berkshire
England
SL6 2QL

email: enquiries@openup.co.uk
world wide web: www.openup.co.uk

and Two Penn Plaza, New York, NY 10121-2289, USA

First published 2012

First published in this second edition 2015

MIX
Paper from responsible sources
FSC® C007785
www.fsc.org

A catalogue record of this book is available from the British Library

ISBN-13: 978-0-33-526178-9
ISBN-10: 0-33-524527-7
eISBN: 978-0-33-526179-6

Library of Congress Cataloging-in-Publication Data
CIP data applied for

Typeset by Transforma Pvt. Ltd., Chennai, India
Printed by Bell and Bain Ltd, Glasgow

Fictitious names of companies, products, people, characters and/or data that may be used
herein (in case studies or in examples) are not intended to represent any real individual,
company, product or event.

The **McGraw·Hill** Companies

Praise for the second edition

For anyone immersed in child protection, there is a requirement to be aware, alert and assertive and to be inquisitive, intrigued, inquiring and imaginative about what children are experiencing when you are not there. These are the powerful messages from this strongly practice-focused text with its emphasis on 'how to do it'. There is clear guidance, and powerful examples, for those still learning their craft and significant reminders for those who are more experienced. There is no more important work than protecting very vulnerable children. This book will help us all do it better.

*Ray Jones, Professor of Social Work, Kingston University
and St George's, University of London, UK and previously
Director of Social Services in Wiltshire, UK*

This is an immensely readable and engaging book, which would have been an enormous resource for me as a practitioner and as a manager of social workers, earlier on in my career. It is written in a succinct, authentic and clear style with practical examples throughout ... Joanna Nicolas brings her commitment to learning from practice alive in this book, drawing on personal examples. Her clarity on issues, such as the legal position of social workers, is excellent.

*Penny Thompson, Chief Executive of the
General Social Care Council (GSCC)*

This book is a gem. Filled with numerous practice-based examples and laced with contemporary, 'real world' dilemmas, it gently encourages practitioners involved in child protection work to think about their work. Whatever their level of knowledge and experience, this book offers excellent, hands-on advice from someone who, clearly, has much experience with families. But what Joanna Nicolas also brings is humanity and a real concern for people: no mean achievement!

David Shemmings PhD, Professor of
Child Protection Research

Five Star Amazon Reviews:

As a team manager for a social work team, I think this is a great book that I will use with unqualified, student and newly qualified social workers who are undertaking ALL home visits...Overall, a great resource that I predict will become my new bible.

The author's very human, honest and self-effacing approach to writing this book is refreshing... Every community practitioner caring for children and families should carry this book with them.

Contents

How to use this book

This pocket book is designed to help guide you through the process of visiting families in their homes in cases of child protection. It can be dipped in to as needed – it does not have to be read from cover to cover and provides a range of complementary yet stand-alone aspects of conducting the home visit.

This is an extremely practical guide and some chapters include checklists on things such as how to prepare for a visit, what to take on the visit, how to make the most of your visit and how to keep yourself safe. There are examples of good and poor practice, case examples drawn from my own experience and that of others, and quick links to research.

Chapter 1 sets out what needs to be done in preparation for a visit. It is essential to be well prepared before you visit someone's home and the reasons for this are made clear in this chapter.

Chapter 2 gives tips and guidance on keeping yourself safe when conducting a home visit. Personal safety must always be a priority when conducting a home visit and should never be forgotten. Use your common sense in this situation.

Chapter 3 looks at how to gain access to the home. You may wonder why you need a chapter on this topic, but obtaining entry can be a tricky part of a visit and this chapter will give you tips and advice on how to be successful in this.

Chapter 4 sets out what you need to do once you are in the home. It will help you consider where to place yourself in a room, where you should be going in the home and who you need to talk to, while emphasising the need to keep the child as the focus of why you are there.

Chapter 5 gives guidance on what to look out for in the home, including possible signs of abuse or neglect. What is the state of the home? How does the child present, the adults present, and how do the two interact? The chapter stresses the need to use your observational skills. Once in the home, utilising these skills is absolutely key.

Further reading and resources can be found at the back of the book to help maintain and develop your practice. These consider both your overall knowledge base and your specific report-writing skills. They are intended to give you some initial signposts to further reading and resources that can be accessed.

There is also a glossary, and glossary terms are shown in bold on their first occurrence in the text. The use of jargon in this book is kept to a minimum but there is some professional terminology that needs to be understood. These terms are explained in the glossary but it also goes further than that, setting out to explain legal terms and **common themes found in child protection**.

The overall aim of this book is to provide you with a flexible and accessible resource that can help you when you are conducting home visits.

Acknowledgements

This book is dedicated to my mother, who is the most exceptional person I know. Without her unwavering love, support, interest and encouragement I would not be in the position I am today. I must also thank my children for putting up with me, and the friends and colleagues who have supported and encouraged me in this project – in particular, Rebecca Kay, James Lovell, Jane Bee and Mark Little. Thank you all.

Setting the scene

This is a book for social workers and other professionals who visit homes in difficult circumstances. I wrote this book as a social worker but there are many other professionals who have to visit people's homes and this can be very challenging work. Therefore, this book is for all the social workers, health visitors, community family workers, education welfare workers, teachers, police and anyone else who is responsible for the welfare of children.

I was delighted to be asked to write it because a practical guide dealing with what to do on a home visit had not been written previously. As a student and a newly qualified social worker I would have benefited greatly from a practical guidebook like this, something I could keep in my bag. At university I learned the theories, I studied the research, but little practical guidance was given. What do you do when you go to visit a family for the first time, and you knock on the door, the door opens and you smile warmly and say, 'Hello, I'm Joanna Nicolas, and I am a social worker', and the response is to be sworn at and the door slammed in your face?

But this book is not just for newly qualified staff. If you are a student or newly qualified worker, it will complement and supplement the theories you have learned, improve your study and help you turn theory into practice. It can also be used by more experienced practitioners, as it will consolidate what you do in your practice. Life is a continuing learning process and if anyone thinks they know it all, I would question their practice. We should all be learning all the time.

> ✓ **Good practice point: We never know it all**
>
> At one point in my career I had a five-year career break, to have my children. The first meeting I attended on my return was a **child protection conference**. There was no family member present and during the meeting a drugs worker was telling the conference about all the different drugs the mother in the family was using. The worker went through a long list, which included heroin, methadone, crack cocaine, etc., and ended with 'Tudor Rose'. There were about 15 professionals at that meeting and they were all shaking their heads at the gravity of the situation. All I could think was that I did not know what Tudor Rose was – was it a new drug that had come on the market while I had been away? If I owned up to my ignorance, would it be like saying I did not know what methadone was? Eventually I had to ask and the drugs worker looked at me as if I really should not have been there, if I knew so little. Witheringly, she told me it was sherry. Looking round at the other professionals it was clear that none of them had the first idea what Tudor Rose was but no one wanted to show their lack of knowledge. Tudor Rose is extremely affordable sherry, and I did not feel so bad I did not know!

The reason for this good practice point is to emphasise that we never 'know it all'. We should never be afraid to ask questions, whether of the families we work with or of our colleagues. We can all learn, and I hope that this book will help all of you, regardless of your years of experience, to improve your practice, question it if necessary and, most importantly, assist you in the difficult work that you do.

Throughout this book, case examples and good practice points are included. The race and gender of the parents and the children, as well as the age of the children, have been changed to ensure complete privacy for the families and children I have met in the 25 years I have worked in social care, in the UK and elsewhere. Other details have also been changed.

LEARNING FROM SERIOUS CASE REVIEWS

Carrying out home visits is one of the hardest areas of social work. However, it is where most assessments of whether a child is safe should take place. One of the most significant aspects of a child protection investigation will take place in the family home, and yet it can be the most challenging and hostile environment to work in. It is also the place where we find out the most about the child because that is where you will get the greatest sense of what the child's life is like. It is unsurprising that child abuse inquiries report that the evidence is often before the social worker's eyes, when they are in a family home. We just have to know where to look and what to do, to become more curious and questioning, rather than accepting what parents tell us. We should always be asking ourselves, 'What is the evidence that supports what the parent is telling us?' As Ferguson (2009) observes, in some of our most high-profile child deaths – Jasmine Beckford (London Borough of Brent, 1985), Victoria Climbié[1] and Peter Connelly[2] – the signs were there but they were missed. Five-year-old Jasmine Beckford was seen by a social worker during a home visit, but she was watching television and stood up only when her mother and the social worker entered the room. The social worker was in the room for 20 minutes and described Jasmine and her sisters as 'well and happy'. We now know that at that time Jasmine was recovering from a fracture to her thigh. Jasmine was battered to death by her stepfather Maurice Beckford on 5 July 1984. She had been locked in a bedroom with bodybuilding weights tied to her broken legs to stop her moving. When she died, she was emaciated and deformed, she weighed just 23 pounds. She had 40 injuries to her face and body; her ribs were also broken and she had ulcers, burns and cuts to her leg.

In the case of Victoria Climbié, there was one occasion on which a social worker did a home visit. Victoria was sitting on the floor throughout the visit. The social worker's recording said that Victoria was clean, well dressed and playing with a doll. That was the time Victoria was kept tied up in the bath. She was doubly incontinent because she was so frightened, and she was kept in a bin bag because of her incontinence. The reason why she was sitting on the floor during the visit was because she could not stand up straight as she spent most of the time tied up. Victoria died of hypothermia because the bathroom she was kept in was freezing. She had 128 injuries on her body when she died on 25 February 2000.

In the case of Peter Connelly, it is well documented that a considerable number of home visits were done by social workers and other professionals. It was noted that the home was in a poor state, that Peter often had bruises and, on one occasion, his face was smeared with chocolate and he had cream on his head. During that visit it is understood the social worker asked the mother to clean his face, a friend took him out of the room but did not return him. Those home visits could certainly have been put to better use in the efforts to protect Peter. He had more than 50 injuries on his body when he died on 3 August 2007.

What came from the **serious case review** for Hamzah Khan, the little boy whose body was found mummified, was this: 'It is now known that five children lived with awful physical and emotional conditions for many months as their mother's emotional and mental well-being was severely impaired and deteriorated.'[3] Many of you will remember the photographs of the inside of the house, the kitchen, corridor, bathroom and bedrooms piled high with plastic bags and rubbish, not a surface visible and virtually no floor space. It is hard to conceive that six people lived in that home. The serious case review author makes the following point: 'The author of the social care report makes an important observation that on the three first visits to the house the various staff only saw the living room. They never saw any child on their own and they never visited bedrooms.' This was five years before the home had deteriorated to the state it had by the time of Hamzah's death. We know from home visits that were undertaken by other professionals that the state of it deteriorated over time.

What came from the serious case review for Keanu Williams,[4] the little boy who was beaten to death by his mother, Rebecca Shuttleworth, after months of horrific cruelty, was that, 'There was no evidence of a child focused process where the Keyworker had been observing the interactions between Rebecca Shuttleworth and the children, or the children in their home environment, to reach an understanding of the children's experience, particularly as they were not able, due to their young ages, to express their views and wishes verbally.' During a four-month period when Keanu and his siblings were the subject of child protection plans due to neglect, there were eight failed home visits. We have to see the home environment and we have to see the children in their home environment with the parents/carers if we are to have the best chance of making an accurate assessment of risk.

These are just four of the terrible tragedies that have occurred when a child has died of **abuse** or **neglect**. As these cases highlight, the signs were there. There is a myth that children who are horrifically abused and neglected are hidden away, unknown to us all. That is untrue. Almost all are known to universal services, i.e. Health Services and/or Education Services, and around half are known to **social care**. This is the evidence that comes from the analysis of serious case reviews[5] undertaken on behalf of the UK government (Brandon, Bailey and Belderson, 2009). This book will help you consider what the signs are, the significance of what is happening in the home, the importance of seeing the whole home and the whole family, and the importance of observing the child within the family context.

The aim of this book is to help you in what is the most essential part of our work, to gain the most from your home visit. Of course, not every family we visit will be hostile, not every home will have an aggressive dog, or menacing men standing around, but a significant number of families we visit will not want us there and that can make it a very challenging environment to work in. This book will address all aspects of the home visit. We can learn so much from visiting the home and it is vital that we use our skills to the best of our ability.

A spotless house and a bulging toy cupboard do not mean there is no risk of neglect, just as a dirty house and a mountain of washing-up do not mean there must be neglect. This book will challenge assumptions, prejudices and stereotypes. The aim is to give you the tools to assess and challenge the families we work with, regardless of their social status.

Example from practice

Many years ago, as a social worker on duty, I was given the unenviable task of contacting a parent whose child was being collected from primary school every day by a babysitter. It had come to social care's attention that the babysitter was taking the child to a pub every day and the babysitter was then drinking heavily and not supervising the child, who would wander around the pub. Clearly there were concerns about this child.

However, the parent did not respond to a letter from social care, so I telephoned the home. The parent could barely contain their fury and disgust that they, an eminent professional, which they were, were being contacted by a mere social worker. The parent made it clear they thought it was absolutely none of our business what arrangements they made for their child, despite my insistence it was a child protection concern and therefore it was most definitely our business. The parent refused to discuss it further and the case was closed after the referrer was asked to come back to us if this continued. Would social care's response have been different had the family been disadvantaged and unemployed?

This book will help you to work through the anxieties you may have. It will help you to find ways of dealing with possible hostility, as well as coping with the pressures of work and time. Ultimately, it will help put you in control. This book will give you the tools to use to establish yourself when you are visiting a family, so you are able to adopt a position of reasonable and non-hostile authority. You are there to do a job but you are also in their home. Social workers must be authoritative without being authoritarian. We are there to listen and to observe.

If there ever was a time for social workers to be saying to their managers that they need to invest the time in a family, it is now. Professor Munro (2010, 2011) has highlighted the need for social workers to have greater autonomy and to spend more time with families, assessing risk. Yet at the same time we have to be realistic about the pressures of work, and the aim of this book is to ensure that you make the most of the limited time you have on a home visit. The quicker we can understand the world from the child's perspective and really know what the risks to the child are, the quicker we can make decisions that are in the best interests of the child. That is best for the child but it also allows us to make more effective use of our time because we will not spend years working with the same family, never really understanding what is going on but never really feeling it is safe to close the case or withdraw our support.

CHILD-CENTRED PRACTICE: RACE, RELIGION AND CULTURE

We work in a time when immigration is high on the political agenda, when multicultural Britain has challenges that bring racism and discrimination, and that can sometimes affect our judgements around child protection.

For example, if a teacher hears of a young Muslim girl who is going to be taken back to her country of origin to be genitally mutilated, the teacher must act. (Apart from the child protection aspect, female genital mutilation is a criminal offence and, under the Female Genital Mutilation Act 2003, it is now a criminal act to plan to take a child out of the UK for her to be mutilated.) A white, British teacher may be afraid to report it because they do not want to be seen to be racist. We must not lose our focus on what the priority is: children's safety and well-being. We have also seen from serious case reviews into child sexual exploitation that a fear of being seen as racist has sometimes prevented professionals from responding. In Rotherham, the inquiry into child sexual exploitation led by Professor Jay[6] concluded that, 'Services did not respond consistently to the cultural needs of minority ethnic communities' and 'By far the majority of perpetrators were described as "Asian" by victims, yet throughout the entire period, councillors did not engage directly with the Pakistani-heritage community to discuss how best they could jointly address the issue. Some councillors seemed to think it was a one-off problem, which they hoped would go away. Several staff described their nervousness about identifying the ethnic origins of perpetrators for fear of being thought racist; others remembered clear direction from their managers not to do so.' The report concluded that, 'There was a widespread perception that messages conveyed by some senior people in the Council and also the Police, were to "downplay" the ethnic dimensions of CSE. Unsurprisingly, frontline staff appeared to be confused as to what they were supposed to say and do and what would be interpreted as "racist".'

The methods recommended in this book put the child at the centre of practice. We must of course be sensitive in our approach and in our work to cultural issues, as well as other issues, but that should never mean we put anything – including considering race, religion or culture – above the protection of children. What we need to do is strip away skin colour, class, race, ethnicity, religion and culture. Every child in this country is entitled to the same level of protection and that is what we have to remember.

USING PLAIN ENGLISH

This book is also 'jargon free'. We are all guilty of using jargon and often use it as a protective mechanism when we are feeling defensive. I will never forget as a newly qualified social worker visiting a parent with an experienced social worker. The parent was a chronic alcoholic, and the children were young and unsupervised much of the time. When we arrived, the parent was slumped in a chair, eyes half-closed, bottle in hand. The senior social worker stood at the door and said to the parent, 'If you don't do something about your drinking, we are going to have to initiate child protection proceedings.' The parent stared at her, with eyes crossed. I struggled to understand what those words meant and I was qualified as a social worker. The parent obviously did not understand. We must beware of jargon.

In this introductory chapter I must own up to my personal bugbear: the use of the words 'appropriate' and 'inappropriate'. They are words that we use all the time that cover a multitude of meanings, so they now are meaningless. If you are visiting someone's house and you tell them you are concerned about their child's inappropriate behaviour, what does that mean? I hope that you will start to notice how often these words come up and how little they mean. What is 'inappropriate sexualised behaviour'? What is 'inappropriate language'? Context and culture are important here.

Example from practice

I was working with a primary school child who had exhibited 'inappropriate sexualised behaviour', according to the school. The school had told the parent about its concerns over this behaviour. The parent did not know what the school meant. Actually what the child was doing was asking teachers if they were virgins. The child was touching teachers' breasts and bottoms and using every possible object as a phallic object. That, and not the blanket statement 'inappropriate sexualised behaviour', tells you about this child's behaviour.

In addition to appropriate and inappropriate I would also add 'attachment' and 'bond'. Again they are words I see written all the time: 'The mother had a secure attachment to her child' is a classic. First of all, a mother cannot have a secure attachment to a child. Unless you would have the confidence to do a presentation on attachment theory to someone who is an expert in the field of attachment, such as Professor David Shemmings, please do not ever use the word. Explain what it is you are seeing, what you are hearing, be explicit. The word 'bond' is cropping up more and more, but just as with appropriate and inappropriate, it is meaningless. Tracey Connelly was described as having a good bond with Peter Connelly. Explain what you see.

Before we move on to the main body of the book, here is just a gentle reminder about the position of power we have when we knock on someone's door, and then when we enter someone's home. It may not feel like it sometimes, but we should put ourselves in the family's position. Social workers in particular have considerable powers and we know that the public's perception is that social workers take children away. We can change families' lives, and whether it is a child protection investigation or an assessment of potential adopters, never underestimate the position of power we are in. That power must not be abused, but at the same time we must not allow ourselves to be intimidated into thinking we are powerless.

So let's remind ourselves why we do this job. Sometimes children need protecting and that is what we are there for. What could be more important than the protection of the most vulnerable in our society? I am proud to call myself a social worker and I am proud of my profession, even if the only time the general public hear about us is when there has been a terrible tragedy involving a child. It is right that we, as a profession, do not retaliate. Our priority must always be the family we are working with, with the child at the centre. We must hold our hands up when our failings have contributed to the death of a child and we must learn from it. We must also bear it when we are unjustly accused because our priority must be the child.

Example from practice

I once heard a mother I had worked with tell her friend that social care had taken her child away because she was epileptic. She also went to the press and this was reported in the papers. Inevitably and understandably, because of that information, social workers were heavily criticised for being so cruel. Aside from the fact that social workers do not have the power to remove children, only the police and the courts can do so, this woman's child had been removed from her care because she was an intravenous drug user who paid for her drugs by acting as a sex worker, and used to take her clients back to her bed-sit where she would have sex with them in front of her young child. That was the reason her child had been removed from her care but what purpose would it have served to have gone to the press with that? Yes, it would have shown social workers in a better light, but this woman was so vulnerable and was a victim of her circumstances. She had been sexually abused as a child. Most of the families we work with are very vulnerable and it is easy to take advantage of that vulnerability.

We must ensure we do the best job we possibly can, in whatever circumstances we find ourselves, and focus on what matters: the protection of children. My aim is that this book will help you do that.

Preparing for the visit

How often do you feel unprepared for the visit you are about to do? 'There's no time to prepare'; 'I'm not really sure why I'm going.' Take control. You are a professional, there to do a job. It is your responsibility to ensure you are prepared. What is the purpose of your visit? What do you hope to achieve from the visit? What factual information do you require? What information do you already have?

This chapter will look at the vital preparation necessary to get the most from the home visit, even if all that means is sitting in your car for five minutes composing yourself before you go in. You will find that time spent in preparation saves time later on; it will also ensure you get the most from the visit. Use the checklist on p. 27 to tick off what you have done in preparation. Whether you are a beginner or an experienced worker, there is no doubt that the more organised and better prepared you are, the more time-efficient you can be. That can only be a good thing.

WHAT TYPE OF VISIT IS IT?

There are different considerations, depending on what type of visit it is. This chapter will look at the different types of visit and what needs to be done in preparation for each one. We will focus primarily on arranging the initial visit, but will also be considering the importance of unannounced visits.

■ *The initial visit.* You will need to consider how best to arrange the visit. Does the family speak English? Are they literate? Should you telephone to arrange the visit? Are there safety issues you need to be aware of? What is the purpose of the visit?

■ *The joint visit*. We do joint visits for a number of reasons. It may be that there are safety issues and it is thought unwise to visit alone or because you want a second opinion on what you have previously witnessed in the home. It may be that you are visiting with the police, who are going to arrest someone, and you are there to ensure the children's safety and well-being. Or you and another agency have decided that a joint visit would be beneficial, for any number of reasons. Perhaps you are going to be discussing something very painful for the primary carer and it is thought to be important for them to have some support.

■ *A follow-up visit*. When you do your initial visit, it is important to establish the best way of arranging visits with the family in future in terms of how you make contact with them, whether there will be an interpreter present, who will read any reports if the family is not literate. You will also need to think about whether future visits should be with another worker, if you are concerned about your safety. This should be discussed with your manager. You will also need to be clear about the purpose of future visits. What are you there to do and what do you need from subsequent visits? (It is too easy to 'do a visit', to tick the box saying you have done the statutory or mandatory visit, but you need to think about why you are there.)

■ *An unannounced visit*. There are situations that merit an unannounced visit. This may be necessary if we believe a family is being dishonest with us about who is in the home, who is caring for the children, whether someone in the home is misusing substances, etc.

Regardless of whether you are visiting under **s.47 of the Children Act 1989** (i.e. undertaking a child protection investigation) or it is thought to be a child in need case, under **s.17 of the Children Act 1989**, always be clear as to why you are visiting. What is the purpose of the visit? What do you need to achieve?

What has come from two serious case reviews I have been involved in recently is that professionals can be more accepting of information when they are working under s.17, without testing it out. Social care

are involved because of concerns, and for social care to be involved the concerns will have had to be significant. We should be equally questioning and test out information, regardless of whether we are working under s.47 or s.17.

Whatever the kind of visit, you need to think ahead and be well organised.

THE INITIAL VISIT: GETTING IN TOUCH WITH THE FAMILY

First of all, what is the best way of getting in touch with the family? Remember that your relationship with the family starts from your first contact with them. Is it better to write a letter and put it in the post, or drop it off yourself? (The advantage of dropping the letter off yourself is that you know it arrived at the home, which is always helpful if a family denies having received the letter.) Or is it better to telephone the family? We can decide on the best way to contact a family only once we have considered the following factors.

■ *Does the family have a history of avoiding contact with social care?* If we know the family is good at avoiding social care, and if we write a letter and post it, and the family denies receiving that letter, there is no proof they did so. Therefore, it would be better to drop the letter in personally, or telephone. That way you have evidence you did make contact.

■ *Does the family speak English?* The person who made the referral should be able to tell you that. If they do not speak English, or only the children do, then it would be best to contact them by letter and the letter must be in the family's own language.

■ *Do you need an interpreter?* You may need to arrange for a letter to be translated and you may need to arrange for an interpreter to accompany you on your visit. If you need to use either service, make sure the person you use is from a professional body, not a helpful neighbour.

> ✓ **Good practice point: Poor practice**
>
> I was once working with a Japanese family. There were considerable concerns that the children were neglected and physically uncared for. The mother's English was very limited and we had some difficulty finding an interpreter. Eventually I came across a voluntary organisation that said it could offer us a service.
>
> During my first visit with the interpreter, I soon realised that something was amiss. Now, my Japanese is not impressive but I started noticing that for every sentence I said, the interpreter would 'translate' longer, for several minutes. Eventually I realised that he was translating and then commenting on what I was saying and adding his own opinion about the mother's neglect of the children. Of course, I could not continue and I came away from that house knowing that I had added to this mother's troubles because I had brought someone into her home from her own community and had shared with them some intimate details about her difficulties.
>
> This is an example of very poor practice, which I am ashamed of, but have never repeated.

- *Is the family literate?* Again, check if the referrer knows, or other agencies involved with the family. If you know the family is literate, you can then make the decision on whether it is best to write or telephone to arrange the visit, based on the other factors. If you know the family are not able to read and write, then you will need to telephone to arrange the visit.
- *Does the family know a referral was made to social care?* Social care should be checking this with the referrer and advising them that, unless it will result in making someone unsafe, the referrer should tell the family they are making the referral. If the family knows a referral has been made, they will be waiting for you to contact them. There may be situations where it is decided it would not be safe to tell a family a referral has been made to social care – for example, if a six-year-old girl arrives at school, clearly in pain, and tells a teacher that her father has put his willy in her bottom,

there is blood in her underwear and it appears she may have been raped. In that situation the school would definitely not tell the parents that it is making a referral to social care. For all the agencies, the work we do is about protecting children and ensuring their safety. For the police it is also about securing evidence, if it is thought someone has committed an offence. In that situation the school would make a referral to social care immediately and advise them that they had not told the parents they had made the referral. At the subsequent **strategy discussion** it would be decided how the family will be approached.

■ *Is there evidence of an abusive relationship and are you going to put anyone at risk by writing a letter?* As part of any assessment, social care needs to ask other relevant agencies if this is the case. If there is domestic abuse and a domestic abuse agency is involved, it is best to take advice from them about how to contact the non-violent partner. For you, the worker, it is your responsibility to check this out.

■ *Does anyone in the family have learning difficulties, or a disability that you need to be aware of?* Again, check with other agencies that have been involved. If, for example, the primary carer is deaf, you may need to take someone with you who can sign.

Example from practice

A referral had come in from the probation service. It concerned a single child under the age of five, living with their mother and father. The father was extremely violent and had a recent conviction for assaulting his partner, with whom he and the child lived. There was a long history of domestic abuse. It was agreed in the first instance that I should meet with the mother, to ascertain and assess the situation. We would then decide how best to incorporate the father in the assessment we were doing. I was concerned about writing to the mother, or telephoning her, in case her partner saw the letter or listened to the call. I knew that the mother had contact with a local domestic abuse support group and so

> I contacted them for advice. The support group had devised a way to contact the mother safely and I followed the same procedure. This ensured the mother's and the child's safety, which was of course the priority. (In the interests of protecting the vulnerable adults and children we work with, I have deliberately not spelled out the method used.)

We need to take all these factors into consideration when deciding how to make contact with a family to arrange a visit. Once you have the information, you can then decide how best to proceed.

WRITING THE LETTER TO ARRANGE THE VISIT

If you have decided to write a letter, use plain English (if that is the language you are using). Do not use jargon, and please do not use the words 'appropriate' or 'inappropriate'!

Example of a standard letter

[Date]

Dear X,

I am writing to you because, as you know, Mary's school has some worries about her, and James's health visitor is a bit concerned that James is not putting on weight. I would like to come and see you to talk about this and wondered if I could come on ... at ...? If that time does not suit you, please would you telephone me on ... so that we can make another appointment?

Please note that it is important that I come to see you. There may be ways that social care or other agencies can offer you support. At the meeting I will explain to you what the role of social care is.

I look forward to meeting you.

Regards,

[Signature]

So the message is, *keep it simple*. I would not go into too much detail in a letter and I would definitely not give reassurance that there is nothing to be worried about, because that may be misleading for the parent. It is one of the dilemmas we face. We ask families to be honest and open with us and then, when they are, it sometimes results in us having to remove a child or children after a decision is made by the Court.

ARRANGING THE VISIT BY TELEPHONE

You may have been told that the family does not read or write and, in that case, you should telephone the family to arrange the visit. It would not be fair to write a letter to a family, knowing they were not able to read it. They may well show it to someone who is able to read it to them and that person will then know their private business.

Example of a telephone call to arrange an initial visit

You: Hello. Could I please speak to X? [Use first name and second name.]

Service user: Who is it?

You: My name is Joanna. Is X there? [Or if it is a mobile, 'Is that X?']

[Do not give more than a first name until you have established who you are speaking to. Nor should you say where you are calling from, until you know you are speaking to the service user.]

Service user: So what if it is?

You: I'm sorry, but I really need to know who I am speaking to before I explain why I am calling. Is that X?

Service user: Yeah.

[You need to decide how you are going to address them. You will not know if that person would prefer to be addressed formally, or by their first name. We should not presume to call someone by their first name, unless

---

we have asked if we can do so. I would therefore suggest that, in most cases, you address the person as Mr/Mrs/Ms.]

You: OK. My name is Joanna Nicolas and I am a social worker. I work for … The reason I am calling you is because I would like to arrange to come to see you to talk about Mary and James. As you know, the health visitor and the school have been a bit worried about the children and I just need to come to see you to talk about it and also to see whether there is anything we can do to help.

Service user: I don't need any help from you.

You: That is fine but I do need to come to see you because the school and the health visitor have passed on their concerns to us, and so a social worker has to come to see you and the children. I was wondering whether I could come on … at …?

Service user: I don't want anyone coming round. You are not taking my children off me.

You: Ms X, I am not coming round to take your children away, but I do need to come to see you. Now, what about …?

Service user: Why can't we do it over the phone?

You: Because I need to come to see you at home and talk to you, and see the children. Now, what days are best for you?

Service user: I can't do Mondays.

You: That's absolutely fine. What about Tuesday at 4 pm?

Service user: If you must.

You: Thank you. Now what I will do is send you a text with my name and number and when I am coming to see you. If there are any problems, please would you give me a ring and let me know? Thank you for your time, Ms X, and I look forward to seeing you on Tuesday at 4 pm.

There are different levels of literacy, therefore send a simple text with the date and time and your name, and remember to use a mobile only if it is a work mobile. It is unprofessional to share your personal mobile number with **service users**; it may also put you in a vulnerable position if the service user ever makes a complaint against you and it is discovered you have shared your personal details with them.

Again, keep it simple, just as you would with a letter. Keep the conversation quite brief. Do not allow yourself to be drawn in to talking about the concerns on the telephone. Take control of the conversation, be courteous but firm.

You need to arrange a date and a time to suit you both, but if you feel the service user is prevaricating, take control.

If the service user puts the telephone down on you and then switches their telephone off, you will need to let your manager know you have been unable to reach them and decide on the next course of action.

GATHERING THE INFORMATION YOU NEED

■ *Does the referrer know you are contacting the family?* Again, social care should have made it clear to the referrer what is going to happen next, and whether social care is going to visit the family. If you are the worker doing the first assessment, it is your responsibility to let the referrer know what is happening.

■ *Is there a potential risk to you?* This is one of the reasons why it is essential to read the file. Is there any evidence that anyone in the home is potentially violent? This must be considered in light of the subject you will be discussing with the family. Should you be visiting alone? Should you be visiting the home at all? You need to weigh up the risks. Unless the situation is so grave that social care are going to seek an emergency protection order, or the police are going to take the child into police protection, seeing the child in the home is an essential aspect of any assessment of risk. However, this must be balanced against the potential risk to you. What you need to consider is that if workers are unwilling to go in to a home because of concerns for their own safety, how can it be a safe place for a child to be?

■ *What do we mean when we talk about 'doing a risk assessment'?* In this context we are talking about whether it is safe for you to visit the home. This book is about child protection and therefore the police will have been involved in the strategy discussion. You need to know, before you do a visit, whether the family is known to the police and whether there are any concerns relevant to your visit, such as violent assaults or drug dealing from the property. If you have concerns, these should be discussed with your manager. You should always be looking to minimise risk, while accepting that it is vital to see a child in her or his own environment. It may be that taking another worker with you reduces the risk. If you are visiting alone, make sure you have a mobile with you and, if you need to, have it on but keep it on silent. It is your responsibility to ensure your employer knows of your whereabouts.

 Reminder: Official policy on lone working

Different employers have different policies on lone working and staff safety. As a general rule, if you are concerned about your safety, discuss it with your manager.

Example from practice

I once had to meet with a father whose partner had recently left him due to the high level of violence. She had gone into a refuge in another area. All this happened without his knowledge because of his threats to kill his partner and his child if she ever left him. These threats were taken extremely seriously, particularly in view of his history of violence and substance abuse.

As the children's social worker I had to tell the father that social care was going to apply to the Court for an **interim care order** for the child and we were going to recommend to the Court that he have contact with the child only when supervised by a social worker.

> In view of what I was going to be telling him and his history of violence, it would clearly be unsafe to visit him where he was living at the time. It was agreed I would see him in a neutral venue, with a colleague and with police back-up, in case he became violent. The police officers were not visible but it was reassuring to know they were there, if need be.

- *Read the file*. This is essential. Time will always be an issue for us, but if you visit someone's house and you have not read the file, you may have missed some essential information that may impact on your safety, as well as the child's. If there is a lot of information on the file, skim-read it. Pick out the essential assessments, reports, etc. Some local authorities are starting to use chronologies. This is because they can be a very effective tool to see what is actually happening within a family. I would always advocate the use of chronologies, particularly multi-agency chronologies. They do keep us focused on the evidence, as opposed to what we are being told by some families, and sadly the two do not always match up.

- *Speak to other agencies*. Best practice would dictate that you speak to all the other agencies involved before you visit. This may not be practicable and in any case if you are doing a child protection investigation, there will already have been a strategy discussion. If you did not attend that discussion, make sure you have read the minutes, or at the very least spoken to the manager who attended.

- *Speak to the previous worker*. If you are taking the case over from another social worker, ask them if there is anything you should be aware of before you visit. This can also be done with other workers – for example, the health visitor.

- *Do you need to take any paperwork with you?* Again, when you are thinking about the purpose of your visit, you should be thinking about paperwork. Are there papers/reports to be read and signed by the family?

■ *Race/ethnicity/cultural issues.* You need to be well prepared. We have already looked at language, but culture is also essential. In this chapter we are looking only at the preparation we need to do before a visit. Therefore, at this point, we are only considering cultural issues in that context. It is common courtesy that we find out what we can about the culture of the family before we visit, so we do not offend. It is also helpful to know for ourselves, so we are prepared. It is not possible to generalise about any ethnic group and therefore it is good advice to mention this aspect when you are asking a previous worker or a worker from another agency, whether there is anything you need to be aware of.

■ *What will you wear?* What you wear is very relevant and should be considered. It is important to remember that we are professionals and there to do a job, so we need to look professional if we want to be respected. But we must also be practical about it and if, for example, you are going to a house where there are small children, you may well be climbed on or find yourself sitting on the floor, so better not to wear a short skirt. It is very important that we do everything in our power to put the families at their ease but if, as is so often the case, it is not just the child who is neglected but also the home, it's hard to appear relaxed about sinking into a sofa that has a seat decorated with squashed Jammy Dodgers, spilled juice and dog hairs if you are wearing your new suit that is dry clean only. A colleague of mine recently found herself removing a hypodermic needle before she could sit down. So wear things you can throw in the wash when you get home, and then you can relax and concentrate on what really matters: the child.

Think about whether it may be helpful to take one or two toys, or a colouring book and pencils. Some homes we visit have nothing for the children to play with and if you take one or two things like this it can be a useful way to build a rapport with a child and also to distract the child while you talk to the parent. I am not suggesting you take a whole toy box, but having one or two things is always handy.

Example from practice

Some of my most embarrassing visits have been when I have been wearing a skirt and boots and I am asked if I would mind taking off my boots. I have a terrible sinking feeling because I realise that I left home in an awful hurry that morning and it suddenly dawns on me I am wearing my son's Star Wars socks. It would be quite wrong to refuse to take my boots off so I sit there talking about child abuse with bare legs and Star Wars socks. It is not very professional and can somewhat undermine one's authority. I would find it quite hard to take that person seriously. (The same applies if you are wearing tights with a hole or ladder in them.) Keep a spare pair of tights or socks in the car. We have to think of everything!

JOINT VISITS

If you are doing a joint visit with a colleague from your own profession, or another, you need to be clear before you enter the home about your individual roles. If you are unable to have a conversation before you leave the office, the very least you should do is arrange to meet ten minutes beforehand to talk through the purpose of the visit and your roles. (I would suggest you do not park outside the home you are going to. It may be unnerving for the service user to see you both sitting and talking before the visit and, if the family sees you and does have something to hide, you are giving them the opportunity to prepare.) If professionals are unprepared and disorganised, a manipulative service user will use that to play them off against each other.

Good practice point: Working with other professionals

I worked with a mother who appeared to be cooperating with professionals. Her children were subject to child protection plans because of concerns the children were being neglected. Part of the child protection plan was that the mother would attend the baby clinic once a week, to have her baby weighed; this was an area of concern. It was during a conversation in the health visitor's car, just before we did a joint visit, that we realised that the mother was playing one of us off against the other, telling each of us that the other had said that she need no longer take her baby to be weighed. This alerted us, and the other professionals involved, to the fact that she was an extremely manipulative woman and we must therefore work very closely together.

UNANNOUNCED VISITS

Unannounced visits are an essential part of the child protection process. We need to be clear why we consider it necessary with any particular family. I know how I would feel if a professional arrived on my doorstep without warning. (I would always try at least to tidy up when the health visitor was coming. With my first baby, it was an achievement if I was dressed and had done the washing up by 11 am.)

Having said that, we can learn so much from unannounced visits. In the second serious case review in the case of Peter Connelly, the review states: 'The value of an unannounced visit by the social worker was demonstrated in bringing the injuries to Peter to light.'[1]

 Good practice point: Follow your hunch

There are so many examples, but this is one that remains with me.

I was involved in a private law case. Both parents wanted custody of the two children and each said the other was an unfit parent. The judge had ordered that the parents share the care of the children. Each parent would go into great detail about the other's poor parenting, but there was little evidence of this. The father would tell me the mother was a heavy drinker, but every time I visited there was no evidence of this. The home was always immaculate, and the children appeared loved and well cared for. The mother was always welcoming and courteous.

The mother had a full-time job and so my visits were always by appointment. One day, on a hunch, I decided to do an unannounced visit in the early evening. The mother did not see who it was before she opened the door. She was clearly drunk, the house was in disarray and there was no sign of the children. When I asked where they were, she told me they were in their rooms and she would get them. She started going upstairs and I followed her, saying blithely, 'I'll just come with you, if you don't mind. It would be nice to see them in their rooms.' She gave me a filthy look, which I just ignored and carried on smiling. (You have to be very thick-skinned to be a social worker!) There was little she could do, without appearing impolite and she did not want to spoil the façade she had built up from the beginning. When we got to the bedrooms, there were keys in the doors and the children had been locked in.

It is worth pointing out that I felt entirely safe with this woman, in this house. I would never recommend doing what I did if any part of you felt unsafe.

What is a hunch? Professionals often talk about having 'a hunch', or instinctively knowing something. Quite rightly, we need evidence of abuse, but as our experience builds up, so does our expertise. It is the opinion of Duncan Helm, a social work professor at the University of Stirling (and of many others), that child protection workers should be encouraged to rely more on gut instincts and intuition. So what does that mean? If you think there is something going on that the family is not telling you, test out your instinct. We should do this in all our child protection work, but in the context of home visiting, do the unannounced visit, ask to see the whole house, look in the fridge as well as the cupboards.

Example from practice

I was visiting a family regularly and there were considerable concerns about the parents' drug use and worries that they were

> spending their money on drugs, not food for the children. The children were very underweight. On my first visit I had asked to see what food they had and they showed me two cupboards full of tins and packets of food. There was not a lot of fresh food, but at least there was food.
>
> This was not fitting with what the children were saying at school and nursery so one day, on a hunch, I picked up the packet of cereal. It was empty. I then picked up a tin and that was empty too. It turned out the family had kept all these tins and packets to show professionals how much food they had, but they were all empty.
>
> Some of the families we work with will be very deceiving and we need to think the unthinkable.

Undoubtedly we will learn more from an unannounced visit and, while it would be wrong to encourage workers to be devious, if there are concerns about who is in the home, or visiting the home, it may be worth stepping aside when you have rung the bell and not being in full view before the door is answered. In the case of Peter Connelly, professionals were unaware of who was living in the home and yet Peter and his two siblings were subject to child protection plans, and considered to be at risk of physical abuse and neglect. Following Peter's death, his mother Tracy Connelly, her boyfriend Steven Barker and her lodger, Mr Barker's brother Jason Owen, were all convicted of causing or allowing the death of a child. All had been living in the house, along with Mr Owen's girlfriend and his children.

Good practice checklist

Things to take with you on the visit:

✓ pen and paper
✓ diary
✓ mobile (with battery charged)

✓ if there are specific questions for the family it is helpful to have those written down, so you can be sure you have asked them
✓ is there any paperwork you need to take?
✓ one or two toys or books, or colouring pencils and paper
✓ a brief list of all the information you need and the questions you need answers to, to make sure you do not forget anything
✓ if you have any leaflets that explain any of the possible processes, or where the families can gain support, take those with you too.

Checklist of things to do in preparation

✓ Read the file.
✓ Speak to other agencies.
✓ Speak to previous workers.
✓ Do an assessment of risk.
✓ Make sure the relevant person in your team knows where you are going and what time you will be back (see Chapter 3, on personal safety).
✓ Telephone the family to confirm the appointment. Be friendly – say you are looking forward to seeing them, or something similar.
✓ If you are doing a joint visit, make a plan with your co-visitor before you go.
✓ Be 100 per cent clear in your mind about the purpose of your visit, why you are going, what you need to achieve, what information you need to gather.
✓ Find out if there are any racial/ethnicity/cultural issues, such as language.

I hope that this chapter has persuaded you of the need to be prepared, however little time you have. If you forget to take the paperwork, you will have to go back and that will take more time. If you were in such a rush that you did not remember to ask an essential question, you may have to go back. However much pressure we are under, ultimately we are all responsible for our own conduct. Part of being a professional is recognising one's own capabilities and limitations, and acknowledging these with our managers. The manager may not be able to decrease your workload, but he or she may be able to help you to manage your time better, and at least the situation will have been acknowledged and recorded. You will achieve better results and feel so much better if you are in control.

3 **Keeping yourself safe**

This chapter will give you some practical tips to keep yourself safe when home visiting, based on my experiences and those of others around me, over the past 20 years. Experts in this field, such as Ray Braithwaite, have written a lot on this topic, so please refer to the 'Further reading and resources' section if you wish to expand your knowledge base.

As any child protection social worker will tell you, we are often in situations where adults, and sometimes children, are hostile and aggressive. I have never been physically assaulted, but I have had my life threatened and been verbally abused and sworn at on many occasions.

We never know when a situation may turn nasty and so we always need to be aware of that when we are going into people's homes and discussing a very sensitive subject. We know that many of the parents we work with will be perpetrators or victims of domestic abuse, many will be misusing substances and many will suffer mental ill-health. None of these factors automatically leads to violence, but may well exacerbate an already delicate situation.

As I will say throughout this book, we need to be prepared. Fore-warned is forearmed. The more we know about the people who live in the home, the better prepared we will be.

It is not just our responsibility to keep ourselves safe. Our employers have responsibilities too. There is also health and safety legislation. If you feel it is putting your safety at risk to visit a particular home alone, or even with another worker, you need to make that clear to your manager. There is an element of risk in the work we do and that is unavoidable. In the words of Professor Munro (2011), we need to be 'risk aware, not risk averse'. Professor Munro is actually talking about the risks we have to take in child protection work, but it is just as true for us when we are visiting people's homes.

It is clearly not realistic to repeatedly voice that you do not want to go into particular homes as this is such a core part of the social work role. However, if there is a genuine case for not visiting a home, either alone or with another professional, you must state your case. It can be very hard to stand your ground; the team is busy, there is too much to do and you are 'making things difficult' by saying you want someone to go with you. A good manager will accept that and support you. However, you may not always have a good manager. Do not allow yourself to be railroaded if you are genuinely concerned.

Reminder: One rule for the child, one for you?

You should also ask yourself why it is OK for a child to be living in the home when you and other professionals are too afraid for your personal safety to visit it. You should raise this with your manager, particularly if you are thinking about panic buttons and 999.

Example from practice

I was working with a family where the children were living with an uncle who was known to be extremely violent. He had spent many years in prison and was well known to the police. He was a perpetrator of domestic abuse, he had assaulted many individuals, including police officers, and he self-harmed, often deliberately cutting himself when in stressful situations with professionals. He was also an alcoholic.

On his release from his latest prison sentence it fell upon me to tell him we had a court order in place. The court had decided he was only to have supervised contact with his nephews and nieces, whom he had brought up.

I was not prepared to see this man on my own, or to visit him somewhere where my safety could not be guaranteed. It was agreed that two of us would see him in a room with two exits and we took everything out of the room except the chairs we were sitting on – we knew he had a propensity to throw things at people when under pressure. We also had four police officers hidden nearby. (He did not like police officers and often reacted violently towards them and therefore they needed to remain hidden.)

As is so often the case in these situations, by the time he arrived my heart was racing and I expected a huge, furious man to come bursting in, swearing and throwing punches. The reverse was true. It was the first time I had met 'Pete' and when I went in to reception to collect him, there stood a small, dejected man. Meeting Pete that day reminded me that many of our perpetrators are victims too. He had grown up in a brutal house, his parents were both alcoholics, there was domestic abuse, and he was a victim of physical abuse and neglect.

The meeting passed without incident but then it came to who was going to supervise his contact with the children. In the team I worked in at the time it was the role of a family support worker to supervise contact, however in this case we agreed that would not be safe. My manager wanted me to do it but I was not prepared to because of concerns for my personal safety. I am a mother and my priority was to keep myself safe for my children. That is not to say that only parents should have regard to their personal safety, or greater priority, but I felt I had to ensure that my children came first and I was adamant I would not do it. I felt very guilty about my decision – I was depriving the children from seeing their uncle, I was making things difficult for my team manager, but I stood my ground.

In the end the team manager supervised the contact sessions, which is highly unusual, and they passed without incident until Pete stopped coming.

There are many definitions of violence. The Health and Safety Executive defines violence as 'Any incident, in which an employee is abused, threatened or assaulted by a member of the public in circumstances arising out of the course of employment.'[1] Surveys of social workers tell us that verbal abuse and threats of violence are common, as they are with some health professionals and others. It is a delicate balance. Abuse comes with the territory, but that is not to excuse abuse or to allow it to continue. We do however have to accept it as part of our job and learn how best to tackle it when it arises.

KEEPING YOURSELF AS SAFE AS POSSIBLE: BE PREPARED

- Find out everything you can about who lives in the home. If you have good connections with your local housing department, that can often be a good way to check if there have been any reported incidents of antisocial behaviour at that address. You will not need to do this for every single home you visit, but it can enhance information you already have if there are already some concerns.
- In all cases you should make sure your team has a good system for checking in, and if there is not one in place, make it happen. Do not forget, your employer has responsibilities too. Many teams have large boards on which staff write down where they are and when they are due to return. If your writing is illegible, like mine, make sure you write clearly. (I used to have a team manager who would write 'R.I.P.' at least once a month in her slot, when she was out of the office. It always looked rather gloomy but actually it stood for 'Research in Practice' and these were monthly meetings she would attend.) Be clear about where you are going and who you are seeing.
- Again, many teams have a 'buddy' system, someone you always check in with, to ensure you are back safely. Be proactive, be the one to set systems up, if they are not already in place.
- Make sure your mobile is charged. If you are visiting somewhere that does not have mobile reception, there may be a greater argument for doing a joint visit, if you are concerned about your safety.

- If you are visiting somewhere you are not sure is safe, try to do it in daylight hours in the winter and do not do a visit you are concerned about at the end of the day when all of your colleagues will be going home.
- If you are visiting a big estate where there are lots of tower blocks, it can be quite intimidating. Try to find out exactly where you are going before the visit, rather than wandering around looking lost.
- If you know there is domestic abuse, it may be helpful to find out when the perpetrator is not there, in the first instance. It will be more likely you could have an honest and open conversation if the controlling partner is not there.
- Think about how you present yourself. Apart from the professional aspect, if you needed to, could you run in the clothes and shoes you have chosen to wear?

 Reminder: Don't ignore the father

If the perpetrator of the domestic abuse is the father, we must not ignore fathers; research from serious case reviews[2] tells us that fathers are often overlooked. Even if the father is the perpetrator of domestic abuse, by avoiding the father and only visiting in his absence, we may feel (or be) safer but it will mean our risk assessment for the children we are there to protect will be incomplete.

JOINT VISITS

As stated in previous chapters, there can be many reasons why we do a joint visit with another professional. This chapter considers a joint visit only from a safety point of view.

The key point is, we are less physically vulnerable if there are two of us, and most people are less likely to be intimidating, threatening or violent if there is a witness. However, there are always exceptions to every rule. Two colleagues of mine were assaulted by a service user when they visited her home together.

Make sure you have a plan. Discuss what you will do if the service user becomes aggressive. It may be helpful for you, the social worker, to deal with the issues that bring you there – leaving your colleague to deal with any hostile behaviour.

Consider where you park your car. If you are visiting a large estate, people may have learned who you are and what car you drive. Park somewhere so that your car can be seen from the window – one of you can then keep an eye on the car, while the other, probably you as the social worker, goes about the visit.

ONCE IN THE HOME

Think about where you are in someone's home. Make sure you sit near the door, so you can leave – quickly if you have to. A good tip is to let the service user lead the way into the room, so that they will take the chair furthest away from the door. You can then sit in the chair nearer the door. Social workers (and other professionals, I am sure) have been known to climb out of windows. It is easier to use the door.

Be mindful of any items around you that could potentially be used as weapons. You cannot guard against everything, but I do remember asking a service user if he would mind removing the samurai sword that was sitting on the kitchen table.

Make sure you have an exit strategy if the situation becomes too dangerous. There are many different ways of doing this. I would suggest you are honest and straightforward, and address any threatening behaviour straight away. Keep it very simple and say something like:

> I can see you are extremely angry and we cannot carry on with this meeting while you are so cross. I am also not prepared to be shouted

at. I am going to leave now and I will telephone you later, when you have had a chance to calm down, and we can then discuss what is going to happen next.

 Reminder: Be assertive

Remind yourself you are there to do a job, but there is absolutely no reason why you should allow yourself to be threatened or shouted at.

Example from practice

I went to see a mother to talk about her 13-year-old daughter, who was making herself vulnerable by associating with older men who were considered to be a risk to children. The mother appeared to have little interest in her daughter's whereabouts and wanted to talk about her own housing problems. Each time I turned the conversation back to her daughter, she became more irate until finally she leapt up, came over to me, leaned over me and shouted at me that she was going to hit me unless I listened to her problems. She also swore at me. I stood up slowly and moved away from her towards the door, calmly telling her I was not going to listen to her if she was going to be abusive. I was going to leave and we would be in touch.

It was only when I was safely in my car that I started shaking like a leaf. It is very frightening to be verbally abused and physically threatened; see the section below on 'Follow-on actions' if you encounter something similar.

LANGUAGE

We have to take some of the responsibility for what happens during a home visit. Professionals can be quick to blame the family, but we also have a part to play. The language we use is so important. I have already warned against using jargon. If your defence mechanism is to use jargon, and you become increasingly defensive, you may use language the service user does not understand and that will only inflame the situation.

You must not allow yourself to become angry when confronted with an angry service user. If you become angry too, it will only inflame the situation. Try to remain calm and assertive.

As Ray Braithwaite says, 'Leaving is always an option. Leave by deception ("I'll just need to get my diary from the car"); walking away positively; making a statement to assist ("Let's take a break") or even running if necessary.'

FOLLOW-ON ACTIONS

All threats should be taken seriously and reported to your manager. Your organisation's procedures should be followed to ensure that the correct response, according to the level of threat, is taken. You will also need to consider the impact on the child. It may be that it was only during the visit you realised how abusive and intimidating a parent was. You need to be discussing with you manager how it made you feel and how it must make the child feel living in that environment, and what action you need to take.

Remember too that, just as it is OK to say you do not know something, it is also OK to say you were scared. It is your organisation's responsibility to ensure you are safe at work, but as well as that I believe the best sort of debriefing is often done with our team members. Strong, supportive teams produce happy, healthy workers. We always hear about the sick sense of humour of those working in crisis situations. Humour can be a wonderful coping mechanism for reducing distress created by stressful situations. You are not a better person for internalising the stress of your job. You are not weak if you say you are frightened. There is so much said about workers becoming 'burned out'. I believe that, if we look after ourselves and each other, there is much less chance of that happening.

Reminder: Be alert

Be prepared, be alert and report any concerns. That is your best chance of avoiding situations that become dangerous.

Good practice checklist: What to do to keep yourself safe

- ✓ Make the appointment during daylight hours in the winter, if possible.
- ✓ Let the office know where you are going and when you will be back.
- ✓ Let your 'buddy' know.
- ✓ Take your charged mobile and pre-program in 999 and your office number.
- ✓ Let people know when you have left the home, so they know you are safe.
- ✓ Finally, use technology. There are an increasing number of apps that track where individuals are. In some situations this may be a useful tactic. Carry a personal alarm and, if you are particularly concerned, have 999 as the last number you dialled before you visit, so it will be quicker than ringing the number again.

4   Getting in the door

We have to be realistic about the fact that many of the families we visit do not want us there. Many families will have a real fear that we are going to take their children away and therefore physically getting in through the door may not be as straightforward as it seems.

Point of law: Removal of children from their parents/carers

Only the police and the courts have the legal power to remove children from their parents/carers. The police can take a child into police protection if they have 'reasonable cause to believe' that the child would otherwise suffer **significant harm** (s.46, Children Act 1989). This protection lasts for 72 hours; otherwise social care would apply to the Court for an **emergency protection order** (s.44, Children Act 1989). An emergency protection order lasts for eight days and can be extended for a further seven days. If it is not deemed to be an emergency, social care would apply to the Court for an interim care order (s.38, Children Act 1989). An interim care order will last for eight weeks and will then have to be renewed.

Social workers do not have the legal power to remove children.

This chapter will look at what to do when the family allows us in and what to do when the family is hostile and tells us to go away. It is important to bear in mind that the family that welcomes us with open arms is not necessarily the one that is treating its children well, and the family that is hostile and resistant is not necessarily the one that is abusing its children.

In your preparation for the visit you should have been able to ascertain whether there are any issues of personal safety to consider and planned accordingly (see Chapters 2 and 3). If the family is known to other agencies, you may have some idea as to whether they are generally amenable to working with professionals, though when faced with professionals working in child protection, the reaction may be very different. Any information you have should affect how you actually physically approach the property.

Good practice point: General guidance

- When the door is opened, only give your first name until you have established who you are speaking to. Then ask for the full name of the person you are there to see.
- When the door is answered, always give the first and second name of the person you are there to see. If the woman's name is 'Carol Jones', there may be two 'Ms Joneses', or two 'Carols' in the property, and you could find yourself talking to the wrong one, which would be extremely unprofessional.
- When you are explaining who you are and who you work for, keep it very general.
- Once you know you are speaking to the person you have come to see, explain who you are and who you work for, but use words that will make sense to anyone. If you name job titles and teams/departments that mean nothing to them, it can be irritating or intimidating. For example, if you say, 'I am a community family worker and I work for the children and families team in the Upper Street office', it probably means nothing to most people. Whereas if you say, 'I work in Family Support for Islington Council', it is clear who you work for and you can explain your role when you go in.
- If the person at the door is not the person you are there to see, keep it simple, as in: 'My name is Joanna and I work for Islington Council.' Do not go into any detail of why you want to see the person. You should be discussing their business only with them.

■ If the service user is called and comes to the door but the other person is still there, you should not go into detail without checking the service user is happy to have the discussion in front of someone else.

■ When you have established you are speaking to the right person, always show them your identification.

EXAMPLES OF CONVERSATIONS ON THE DOORSTEP

Non-hostile single parent: Arranged visit

[Door opens]

You: Hello. My name is Joanna and I am looking for Carol Jones.

Ms Jones: That's me.

You: Hello, Ms Jones. I am Joanna Nicolas and I am a social worker. I work for Islington Council. Here's my ID.

Ms Jones: What do you want?

You: Do you remember getting a letter from me, saying I would like to come and see you today at 11 am?

Ms Jones: I can't remember.

You: That's fine, but I wrote to you asking if I could come and see you today about your children, Mary and James. I need to talk to you and I wonder if we could go inside?

It is not always as straightforward as this and we will now consider other situations.

Planned visit to Ms Jones

[Male answers the door]

You: Hello, I am looking for Carol Jones. Is she here?

Male: Who are you?

You: My name is Joanna. I am from the council. Is Carol Jones here?

Male: What do you want?

You: Sorry but it is Ms Jones I am here to see. Is she here?

Male: CAROL! ... There's a lady here from the council. Wants to talk to you.

[Carol then comes to the door and the man remains there.]

You: Hello, Carol. My name is Joanna Nicolas and I work for the council. I would like to have a chat with you but it is rather personal, so I wonder if I could come in and we could talk somewhere privately?

[Do not mention in front of the man that you have written to arrange the appointment. If it is an abusive relationship, she may not have told her partner about the letter.]

Carol: Come in then, if you're going to.

VISITING A HOSTILE FAMILY

If you are visiting a home where you know the family does not like working with professionals, you need to take a different approach. If you are visiting a house, keep yourself as inconspicuous as possible until you are on the doorstep and listen to see if you can hear voices before you knock on the door.

If you are visiting someone who lives in a block of flats, again walk around the side to stop yourself being seen. Professionals often stand out in many of the areas we visit, particularly if we arrive in a car. Ring someone else's bell and ask if they could let you in because you have a letter for number 6 (that should be a random number you have seen, not the flat you are actually visiting). In my experience, someone will always let you in and some blocks have a tradesman's bell that lets you in before a certain time, so it is worth trying that bell first. Before you knock on the door of the flat you are visiting, again listen at the door to see if you can hear voices or activity. By doing this, if all goes quiet when you knock on the door and the family refuses to open the door you have evidence that someone is present in the flat.

Planned visit to possibly hostile family

You knock on the door, having heard noises coming from inside the home. The noises stop, all goes quiet and the door is not answered. After you have knocked again, if there is still no response, call through the letter box. (Do not put your face close to the letter box in case there is an aggressive dog.)

You: Hello, Carol. It's Joanna here, from the council. I need to talk to you but I don't want to talk out here. It would be helpful if you would let me in, so we can talk privately.
[My experience is that at this point the family knows when it is beaten and generally someone comes to the door and lets me in.]

[If the door is answered by the woman you presume to be Carol Jones:]

You: Thank you.
[Said with a big smile and then carry on as in the previous example.]

[If the door is answered by a male:]

Male: What do you want?

You: I am from the council and I am here to see Carol Jones. Is she here?

Male: What business is it of yours?

You: I am here to see Carol Jones. I would be grateful if you would tell me whether she is here, or not.

Male: CAROL! There is some woman here to see you. Get here now!

You then have to make a judgement as to whether you feel it is safe to go in to the home. You should never enter a property if you feel it is unsafe to do so and it would be perfectly acceptable in the scenario above to say firmly, 'I have come here to speak to Carol but I am not going to come into your home because you seem angry. Is everything all right, Carol?' If the male apologises and you consider it safe to enter the property, that is a judgement for you to make on the day. If Carol says everything is fine but you feel threatened by the man, you could arrange for her to come in to the office at a time that is convenient for you both. You would then leave.

 Reminder: You are a professional

It is really important that you remain calm and professional. Do not let yourself be bullied into explaining why you are there. Unless the man is the father of the children – and in this scenario we assume he is not – he has no right to know anything. Keep reminding yourself you are a professional and there to do a job.

If you have had no response to calling through the letter box, you will have to leave, but it is important to put in your recording that you heard noises in the flat before you knocked and that it then went quiet. It all helps to build up evidence.

OTHER SITUATIONS YOU MAY BE FACED WITH

An enthusiastic or aggressive dog

Many of the homes we visit will have a pet dog. The dog might be completely harmless but if you are worried in any way it is perfectly acceptable to ask the family to put their dog away before you enter, or any other pet you feel intimidated by, as long as the way you ask is considerate of the fact that it is their house and you are the uninvited guest. I would simply say, 'I am so sorry but would it be possible for you to put your dog in another room before I come in? I am rather wary of dogs.' In almost all cases the family will do this. In an extreme case they may say, 'It's our house and it's up to us where the dog is. Not you.' In that case you need to become more assertive and I would suggest this as a response, 'I am sorry but I do need to speak to you today but I am very wary of dogs and I won't be able to come in if you will not put the dog in another room just while I am here. Can I just be clear? Are you saying you are not prepared to do that?' Again, you have to feel it is safe to enter a home and if you are too busy worrying about a snarling or licking dog, you are not going to be able to concentrate on what matters – most importantly, that is the children.

If the family refuses to put the dog away, I would simply say, 'I am sorry but I am not going to come in if you are not willing to put your dog away. So I am going to leave now and my office will be in touch.'

I have been in to many homes over the years with a range of pets wandering around that I would not choose to be in a room with – from iguanas to snakes. The most important thing is that you have to focus on why you are there and not be distracted by other things, and if you think you will be distracted, whatever the reason, ask the family, very politely, if they would mind putting the animal away or meeting in another room.

Example from practice: An unsuitably dressed service user

On more than one occasion I have visited a home where the occupant was semi-naked when answering the door. On this occasion I was visiting a father, who knew I was due to visit. It was a hot summer's day and he answered the door dressed only in a small pair of Y-fronts, which, I remember distinctly, had hearts on them. He invited me in and this was how the conversation went:

Him: Hello, Joanna. Do come in.

Me: Thank you, Jim, but I will wait here and give you some time to get dressed.
[In other words, you are giving the impression that you thought he had forgotten your visit and was still getting dressed.]

Him: No. No. It's fine. It's so hot, I was in the garden. Come on through and we can sit outside.

Me: Thank you, Jim, but I would be grateful if you would get dressed first. As you know, I am here to talk about the children and it would be easier to do that if you were dressed. I'll just wait here until you are ready.
[At which point Jim knew I was not going to go in until he was dressed so, defeated, he got dressed and we had a constructive conversation about his children.]

As in this example, it is very helpful at times to use closed statements, but only when working with uncooperative families. We are always taught to use open questions: 'How was your day?' as opposed to 'Did you have a good day?', 'How did you get that bruise?' not 'Did you get that bruise falling over?' However, if you are working with a family with whom you need to be assertive it can be much more effective to use closed statements at times, which leave little room for argument. This does not apply when you are undertaking the investigation, or assessing the level of risk, but only in the context of making appointments, entering the home, seeing what you need to see in the home, etc. In Jim's case, my response to being invited to conduct the interview with Jim semi-naked was 'I will just wait here until you are ready.' If I had ended my part by saying 'Would that be OK?' it gives Jim room to manoeuvre.

Similarly, when you find yourself talking through a letter box, it is much more effective to say, 'Hello, Carol. It would be helpful if you would let me in, so we can talk privately' rather than 'Hello. Is anyone there?'

A child answers the door

When the door is answered by a child, the first thing to do is to ask if mummy/daddy is there. What happens next will depend on the child's response and their age. If the child says 'Mummy's asleep' and it is a young child, I would ask them if they could be very clever and go and wake mummy up, while I wait on the doorstep. If they come back and say they cannot wake her, you need to ensure that both mother and child are all right. If you feel it may be unsafe to enter the home, ring the police and stay there with the child until the police arrive. If you have no concerns for your personal safety, go in to the home with the child, calling the mother's name loudly. If she is in a bedroom, knock on the door loudly and call her name until she wakes up.

Example from practice

I was visiting the home of two children, aged 18 months and three years. The mother was an alcoholic who was working with a voluntary organisation to try to stop drinking. She was a binge drinker and usually binged at weekends while her own mother would care for the children.

It was a precarious situation and the children were subject to child protection plans. We were considering applying to the Court to remove the children because the mother refused to let her mother help more, and she was becoming increasingly hostile towards those trying to help and support her.

I was doing an unannounced visit because I had my suspicions that the mother was doing a good job at covering up what was really happening so that, when professionals did arrange visits, things were not too bad.

When I knocked on the door, the three year old answered. I asked him if he could get mummy, but he said she was asleep. I said, 'Do you think you could be really clever and go and wake mummy up?' He stood there, with his thumb in his mouth and shook his head. I realised that was not going to work, so I said, 'Are there any other grown-ups here?' (I wanted to know what I was walking into.) Again he shook his head, thumb not moving.

What to do?

I knew I could not leave. There were two small children unsupervised and a mother who may have been asleep, unconscious or even dead. I did not consider there to be a risk to myself if I went in alone, so it would have been a waste of police time to call them. I did not call my manager again because I was not concerned about my safety and I knew in this case I had to go in to the home and find the mother, which I did. I went in slowly, calling her name all the time, while talking to the child. We went in to the front room and there was the mother, asleep on the sofa with a large empty cider bottle next to her and a mug of cider on the table. There were several empty bottles lying around and an ashtray full of cigarette ends, with a lighter and matches on the coffee table. The baby was sitting on the floor eating crisps.

I kept calling the mother's name until she woke up. She was still drunk and the first thing she did was tell me to 'p*** off'. I ignored that and offered to make her a cup of tea, which she grudgingly agreed to. This gave her time to wake up without me being there; it also gave me a chance to see what state the kitchen was in and whether there was any food. The kitchen was in a terrible state and there was very little food. By the time I went back in to the front room, the mother had composed herself a bit but was clearly drunk. I was not happy to leave the children alone with her. The baby was weighed down by her nappy and both the children were filthy. I was also concerned that the children had access to matches, a lighter and alcohol that looks like apple juice. I offered to change the baby's nappy, again it needed doing urgently and it gave me a chance to see the bedroom. There was no bedding in the cot, or on the three year old's bed and an open plastic bag full of soiled nappies.

The mother agreed that she was having a bad day and that the children should go to her mother until she felt better. I rang the children's grandmother and she came and took the children.

As always, you have to make a judgement. If there is no adult there, is the child old enough to be left alone? (There is no legal age that a child can be left alone; it depends entirely on the child and the circumstances.) Is it safe for you to enter the home? Should you call the police? Should you ring your manager for advice? Those are your options and you will have to make the decision based on the evidence you have. Figure 4.1 presents the possible choices to be made.

In all of the work we do, we have to constantly consider levels of risk – both to the child, an adult who may be vulnerable and some-times to ourselves. Decisions always have to be made on a case-by-case basis. There are so many variables in every situation that it is impossible to set out every single example of what would be high, medium or low risk. Keep asking yourself, 'What is the impact on the child?', or indeed the adult or yourself. A risk assessment, just as with any assessment, should be ongoing. Factors change all the time.

The person answering the door does not speak English

Once you have established that the person answering the door does not speak English, I would very clearly enunciate the name of the person you are there to see. You could also try writing down and showing them the name. If you get nowhere with this, there is little you can do; you will most probably have to return with an interpreter.

If the person you are there to see comes to the door but they do not speak English, you could try saying 'English?' and gesticulating into

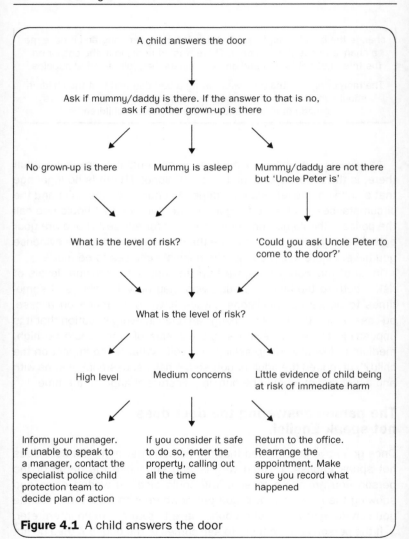

Figure 4.1 A child answers the door

the home. In other words, is there anyone there who speaks English? If no one is forthcoming, you will have to return with an interpreter. If someone else comes forward who does speak English, first of all establish who they are and whether they are related to the children or are the primary carer. If they are not, I would give away very little information. I would ask to see the children and then, depending on the circumstances, I would explain I will return with an interpreter. Try to agree a time with the primary carer then, as it will be difficult to communicate by telephone later.

As in all cases, your decision will depend on the urgency and purpose of your visit. Figure 4.2 presents the possible choices to be made.

Figure 4.2 The person answering the door does not speak English

You are unable to gain entry

If you are unable to gain entry to a home for any reason, your first thought must be about the child you went to see. What is the level of risk to that child? Do you need to report straight back to your

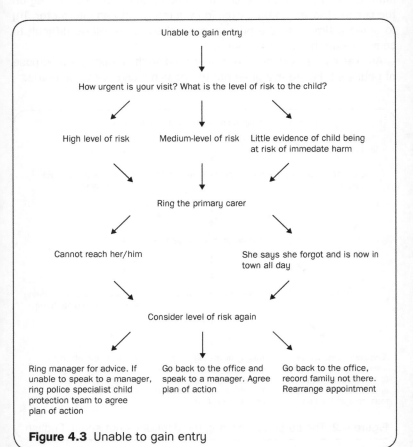

Figure 4.3 Unable to gain entry

manager that you were unable to see the child? (This will depend on the level of risk.) For example, if you are doing the first home visit to a three-day-old baby who is the subject of a **child protection plan** following a **pre-birth child protection conference** and you are unable to see the baby, that must be taken very seriously. Always weigh up the risk to the child when considering your next course of action, and always record when you have been unable to see the child. Figure 4.3 presents the possible choices to be made.

What comes frequently from serious case reviews is that professionals have attempted to undertake home visits but have been thwarted for a number of reasons. In the case of Hamza Khan, the little boy whose body was found mummified, there were eight failed attempts to visit the home, and these were during a period when Hamza and his siblings were the subject of child protection plans.[1]

Good practice checklist: Getting in the door

   ✓ Be prepared for resistance and also for challenging situations so you have a strategy for tackling what you encounter – for example, what you will do if children answer the door, if parents are intoxicated, or how you will tackle a language barrier or other difficulty.
✓ Be assertive and don't go along with anything you feel uncomfortable about.
✓ Do not discuss details until you are sure you are talking to the right person.
✓ Used closed questions if necessary.
✓ Always assess the level of risk when making decisions.

What if you cannot get in?

✓ You need to ask yourself if and why it matters.
✓ Consider the level of risk carefully. If you are satisfied that it is low, arrange a follow-up appointment.
✓ If you feel there are strong grounds for children to be at risk, contact your supervisor and follow the procedure advised by your organisation.

5 Once in the home

We have already established that in some high-profile child deaths professionals had missed some critical and key signs during the home visit. It is vital that we make best use of our time in the home and use all our skills to achieve a better understanding of what life is like for the child living there. This chapter will help to remind us what we are there to do and what our priorities should be.

SETTING UP THE INTERVIEW

Establishing who is in the room

The first thing is to establish who is in the room and who will remain for the interview. You are there to do a job. If the room is full of people, you must say to the person you are there to see that you need to talk to them but would not want to do so with so many others in the room.

Example from practice

A social worker told me recently she was unable to have a satisfactory conversation with a mother during a child protection investigation because there were too many people in the room when she visited, all of whom were joining in. The visit was chaotic and the purpose of the visit – to ascertain the children's safety, in this case – was blurred by the many contributions.

If the room is full of people, you must explain, courteously but firmly, to the person you have come to see that you need to talk to them privately. We cannot 'order' people to leave a room, nor can we insist we see a parent/carer alone but, as with all areas of our work, we have to make a judgement. In the above example, if there are other people coming in and out of the room and expressing their opinions, it may well help us to judge the mood and atmosphere in the home but we will not gain the most from our conversation with the mother. And, as stated previously, we must be careful about disclosing confidential information in front of others.

✓ **Good practice point: Identification**

You have now got in to see 'Carol Jones' and you are in her front room. There are also an older woman and two men in the room. You need to be mindful of the serious case review research that talks of 'shadowy men'. Ideally you should ascertain who these other adults are. You should certainly ask.

You: Thank you for agreeing to see me, Carol. Before we start talking, could I just ask who everyone is?

You: [Looking at 'man 1'] Hello, I am Joanna Nicolas. Could I ask who you are?

Man 1: I'm John.

You: Sorry, John who?

Man 1: John Evans.

You: Thank you, John.

[Repeat this with the other adults, then say:]

You: As I said on the phone, I need to talk to you, Carol, but it is a personal matter and I would like to talk to you privately.

Carol: Anything you say to me, you can say in front of my mates.

You: I am afraid I can't because it is confidential. Is there another room we could go in to, so we can talk privately?

[All this time you need to be pleasant but firm.]

Carol: I'm not moving.

Man 1: Neither am I.

You: Carol, you know I am here because I need to talk to you about the children. I am not going to do that in front of other people because it is confidential information. I need to talk to you privately. If you are telling me you are not prepared to do so, I will make a note of that, however I would really like you to reconsider.

In this example Carol is being hostile and therefore I am being assertive. If I thought Carol was frightened of one or both of the men in the room, I would take a different approach – I would ask them questions first about their involvement with the children and with Carol, and feel my way from there. Either way, we need to be asking who the men are. Men are too often overlooked in child protection work and we need to know who everyone around the child is.

So now you will have established who is in the room and who now remains in the room. You will be beginning to get an impression of what it might be like for the child living in this home and this will become a vital part of your assessment.

Dealing with distractions

In the previous chapter we considered pets and how distracting, or intimidating, they may be. The same can be true of the television. It is not uncommon to find the television on when we visit families' homes. Just as with pets, this may just be how the family does things and the television is always on, but it is very distracting when you are competing with what is on the telly.

As always you must remember that you are in someone else's home so you must always request, not dictate. Ask courteously but firmly if the television could be turned off. You could try something like: 'I'm so sorry but could I ask you to turn the television off? We need to talk about Sam and Lily, and it is going to be difficult to do that with the television on. Thank you so much.'

I then wait until it is off before I carry on speaking, smiling politely but making it clear that the conversation cannot proceed until it is off. Some families will just turn it down and then I say, 'So sorry, but please could you actually turn it off, I really need all your attention.' As professionals you always need to be polite but sometimes you have to be authoritative too. Another feature of serious case reviews is when it comes to light after the child has died or suffered the serious injury that, throughout the professionals' involvement, the parents were calling the shots. Professionals are so mindful of working in partnership with parents that sometimes we forget why we are there. It is a very difficult balance, but we have to keep reminding ourselves that we are there because of real, or potential, abuse of a child and everything must come back to that.

Another distraction is mobiles. I have come to the conclusion we are all addicted to our mobiles, and I have to hold my own hand up as guilty too. Professionals are just as bad as service users, adults are just as bad as children. In the context of home visiting mobiles can be extremely distracting. I hope it goes without saying that yours should be off (with the very few exceptions of situations where you feel yourself to be at risk of harm – see Chapter 2). I have been on visits when another professional has taken a call, and that is appalling. It is telling the service user that the call is more important than this meeting, and you are in their home. If a service user picks up their phone to text or take a call when I am with them, I wait until the end of the call or until the text has been sent and then say something like, 'So sorry, but could I ask you to put your phone away while we are talking. I'm here because of worries about Sam and Lily, and I really need your full attention. I'm sure you think this is just as important as I do.'

All of the distractions I have mentioned may be habitual with the individual or family and there may be nothing more to it. But others will have learned that television or mobile calls make very good diversion tactics, just as bringing a baby to a meeting and dumping them in the middle of the table can be. It is up to you, as the professional, to deal with these distractions, so you can get on with what you are there to do.

Hospitality

Sometimes you will be offered a cup of tea by the service user. It is entirely up to you whether you accept. Frankly, there are some homes we go into where you would not choose to drink out of a cup. In that situation I always say, 'Thank you so much but I have just had one.' Sometimes I hear of professionals going on a visit and taking their coffee they have just bought in a coffee shop. Personally I think that is insensitive. First of all, takeaway coffee is extremely expensive and this can create a barrier with service users who are experiencing hardship, but also it is sending the message that, 'What I have bought is better than what you would have offered me.'

If you need to use the bathroom then it is fine to ask and, also, the bathroom can often be a good indicator of hygiene in the home. I have been in homes where the water has been cut off so the toilet does not work and I have only known how serious the situation is because I asked to use the toilet.

GAINING ACCESS TO THE REST OF THE HOUSE

Just as we do not have right of entry to a property, we also do not have the right to look around the home without the parents' or carers' consent, but how can we do a thorough assessment of the child's situation if we have not seen where they sleep, eat and bathe? It is essential, when we are visiting a home as part of a child protection investigation, that we see the child's environment and, if the family will not allow this, it should make us question why.

Example from practice

Khyra Ishaq was a little girl who lived in Birmingham with her mother, her mother's partner and five siblings. She died in May 2008, and her mother and her mother's partner were convicted of her manslaughter.

When she died, her weight was below the 0.4th centile and she was severely malnourished. Her siblings, who survived, were also severely malnourished. The family was known to health, education, social care and the police. Most professionals who attempted to visit the home were refused entry. In the words of the serious case review:

Living conditions within the household deteriorated over a period of months, it is now known that the mother wanted to be re-housed to larger premises, but was frustrated in this desire by the registered social landlord due to the state of decoration within the home, this in part due to the fact that the children had drawn pictures on the walls. At some point after the partner moved in to the household, the couple began a programme of refurbishment. It would appear, however, that this was not tackled in a systematic way and new projects were initiated before the previous ones had been completed. This resulted in a constant reduction of habitable space within the house, eventually leading to only one upstairs bedroom, which all of the children occupied, a downstairs room which mother and partner shared and access to the kitchen, which was secured with a padlock and only accessible by the adults.

If the police who undertook a welfare visit, or the social workers who attempted to visit, had seen the inside of that house they would have known that the situation was grave.

Example from practice: Daniel Pelka

Daniel Pelka was a little Polish boy who lived in Coventry with his mother, stepfather and siblings. He died on 3 March 2012. His mother and stepfather were convicted of his murder. The conclusion of the serious case review[1] was that Daniel had been suffering abuse and neglect over a prolonged period of time.

Details that emerged from the criminal trial showed that in the house there was a box room from which the door handle on the inside had been removed, so it would not be possible to open the door from the inside. It is thought that the handle was removed on 23 October 2011.

It was known that Daniel was put in this room. Professionals thought that Daniel slept with his sister in a bedroom, which was seen to be clean, with plenty of toys. We will never know how much time Daniel had to spend locked in this room and whether he was there every night. When the room was discovered it contained only a soiled mattress and a damp carpet. There was no heating and no toys, and it smelled of urine.

If professionals working with that family had seen that room it should have been clear that something was not right and that may have helped them to gain a better understanding as to what was happening in this family.

 Reminder: Question everything

If the family is preventing us from seeing the home, then that may be very significant and needs to form part of our assessment.

This is not to suggest that, as soon as you enter the home, you tell the parent or carer you need to see the entire house. That would be insensitive and poor practice, and you should approach any request to see the house with tact – see my suggestions below for tackling this request. However, if you are doing a child protection visit and you have not yet seen the bedrooms, kitchen, front room and bathroom, you need to do so, or record clearly why the parent is not willing to let you see the home.

While you are discussing this with the parent/carer, you must also be mindful of the fact that this is very intrusive. How would we like a complete stranger to go in to our children's bedrooms? Again, this is a judgement call and it should depend on the level of concern. If the concern is that a young child is malnourished, unwashed and with dirty clothes, I would say you should be checking all of the house, as well as the cupboards and fridge for food, and remember to check that the tins and packets do actually have food in them.

Example from practice

I was doing my first visit to a family where the mother was a known substance misuser; she was a single parent with two children under three. Professionals had been involved since her first child was born and there were many concerns about neglect.

Two weeks prior to my visit, two Children's Centre workers had been in and cleaned her house from top to bottom, to show her what was expected of her. (Her home had always been very dirty, chaotic and dangerous for two young children.)

The day of my first visit, as soon as I entered the home I could see it had deteriorated to its previous state. It was filthy and the baby was crawling around in dirt, old food, cat hair, etc. There was nowhere to sit in the sitting room because there were piles of clothes, papers and general clutter on every chair. There was also a low table with cigarette lighters, coffee cups, overflowing ashtrays, alcohol and drugs paraphernalia on it.

In the kitchen there was one packet of biscuits that the two year old was helping himself to and some tea bags – that was it. There was nothing in the fridge, apart from some curdled milk.

Upstairs the children's bedroom smelled very strongly of urine and faeces. There was no bedding on the bed or the cot, only grey mattresses, sodden with urine. There was a bare light bulb swinging from the ceiling, which was accessible from the bunk bed, which had a ladder propped up against it. The mother's bedroom was in an equally poor state and there were cat faeces on the floor. The bathroom and toilet were indescribably dirty, and there was no toilet seat or lid.

If I had only seen the first room I had been taken in to, I would have had no idea about the state of the rest of the house. I could have made *an assumption* about the state of the rest of the house, but that would have been wrong. I needed the evidence.

Only ask to see the rest of the house once you have had a conversation with the family and hopefully built up some kind of rapport with them. I am not suggesting any of this work is easy, and it can be very difficult to ask someone if you can see their bedrooms, kitchen and bathroom, and then if you can look in their fridge and their cupboards, so the next Good practice point gives some suggestions as to how you could phrase the questions.

Good practice point: See the whole picture

■ Say: '*Carol, you know we are worried about the children. Part of what I am here to do is to see how things are at home, for you and the children. In order to do that I will need to see the rest of the house. If we could start with the children's bedrooms and work our way down.*'

■ Remember – never inform a family, when making an appointment to visit them, that you will need to see the whole house, as this then gives them the opportunity to change anything you may find that concerns you. Your assessment must include the child's bedroom.

■ Say: '*Thank you for showing me the bedrooms, Carol. Now if I could just have a quick look at the bathroom.*'

■ Remember: do not overlook the bathroom. Victoria Climbié was kept in the bath and it is often the place where poor hygiene is evident.

■ Say, when in the kitchen: '*Carol, you know that there are worries about the children's weight and what they are eating. I will need you to show me what is in the fridge and the cupboards, to show me what food you have in at the moment. I am sorry I have to ask you to do this but we need to make sure you have enough food and, if you don't, we can help you with that.*'

■ Remember: your immediate concern should be whether the children have food that day or that week. The same would be true of baby milk and nappies. A longer-term concern would be whether the mother has an income and, if she does, what she is spending her money on.

Point of law: A family without recourse to public funds

We must never assume a family is in receipt of benefits if they are not working. Depending on the family's immigration status, they may not be entitled to public funds and this may impact on their ability to care for their children. It is our responsibility to make sure we understand the legal status of the families we are working with and what the possible impact on the children will be.

Reminder: Never make assumptions

Throughout this book I have warned against making assumptions. Do not assume that, because the front room you have been shown in to is immaculate, the rest of the house is too, and do not assume that because you have seen one child's bedroom and have had no concerns, the others will be just the same. A particular child in a family can be scapegoated and treated very differently to the others.

Example from practice

I was involved in an assessment of an uncle and aunt, who had recently had their niece and nephew placed with them in an emergency. They had no children of their own. The children had been living with their father but he took a drug overdose and was admitted to hospital. The children's mother was in prison. She was an intravenous drug user and she was in prison for stabbing the uncle, her brother, who was now caring for the children. The children were aged eight and four, a boy and a girl.

The uncle and aunt had shown great interest in the money they would receive if they were to care for the children, and there were some concerns about their motives. It was my job to assess and then recommend whether the children should remain with their aunt and uncle in the long term.

There were no concerns about the children's school attendance, appearance or appointment keeping. The home was immaculate and the children appeared to be well fed. The trouble was, I had a hunch that all was not as it seemed, but I could not explain why. One day I asked the children to show me their rooms (this was not a child protection investigation, but I knew it would give me greater insight into their lives and them if I saw where they slept and played). First of all, the boy showed me his room – it was overflowing with cars, trains, Lego and books. There was plenty of furniture and it looked like a typical bedroom of a loved and wanted child. I was then taken by the little girl into her bedroom. In it there was a bed and a chair. That was it. There were no toys or books and no other furniture. When I asked her if she had any toys, very reluctantly she went under her bed and brought out two pieces of Lego and a toy that had come free with a meal. (Having worked in this field for a long time, there are not many situations that make me want to cry, but this was one of them. I dug my fingernails into my hands and admired the toys she had.)

What came to light was that the uncle hated the little girl because she looked like her mother. It was her mother who had stabbed the uncle, and in time he admitted that every time he looked at this little girl, she reminded him of the sister he hated and feared. Everything this little girl did was 'wrong', and that included spilling her drink, getting toothpaste on her clothes, wetting the bed. She was four years old and living in fear.

Needless to say, both those children were removed from the home.

TALKING TO THE CHILDREN

We keep seeing from serious case reviews that professionals do not talk to the children and sometimes do not even see them. There may be several reasons for this, the most common given by social workers is that there simply is not time to talk to children. I would suggest, however, that there may be some who are reticent to do so because they are unsure about how to set about it. If we do not feel confident about our ability to do something, we shy away from it, we feel uneasy and intimidated by it, and so we avoid it. The trouble is that if we are nervous about talking to children, it rather loses the point of the work we are trying to do. How can we complete an assessment of a child if we do not talk to the child, observe the child and ask the child what they think? If you read/write in a report 'child seen', what does that actually mean? It is not enough to 'see' a child. We need to communicate with that child. This is a matter of enormous importance and concern, which should be addressed by the workforce.

Example from practice: Daniel Pelka

When Daniel's older sister was interviewed as part of the criminal trial she was able to tell the police some of the things the mother and stepfather had done to Daniel. In the words of the serious case review:

> After Daniel's death, it also became apparent from her evidence that Anna had tried to protect him on a number of occasions, recalling how she had hit out at Mr Krezolek more than once to stop him hitting Daniel or making him stay in a cold bath. Therefore throughout the time from autumn 2011 it was apparent that she was very aware of the abusive experiences of her younger brother but was instructed to say nothing. One of the texts between her mother and Mr Krezolek spoke of the need to remove the door handle from the box room to prevent Anna giving Daniel any food. On one occasion towards the end of January 2012 Ms Luczak told Anna to tell people that Daniel ate more than her and that he needed to be taken to a psychiatrist because he was retarded.

There is no guarantee, but it may be that, had professionals spent more time building a relationship with Anna, she may have felt able to tell them what was happening in the home.

There is a sobering message that is coming very clearly from the serious case reviews and the inquiries into child sexual exploitation. We have not listened to the children who have clearly been telling professionals what is happening. When you are in the home you should be spending as much time with the children as you do with the adults. With older children the home might not be the best place to see them because they may feel more able to talk when they are away from the home where they are being maltreated. We know there are strong links between neglect and child sexual exploitation. Here is a practical checklist to help you to establish good communication with a child.

Good practice box: Talking to the child

- Get down to the child's level, physically. Sit on the floor or sit on a little chair.
- If you are in a young person's bedroom do not presume to sit on their bed. If there is nowhere else to sit, ask before you sit down and, if they do not want you to, sit on the floor.
- Try to think of yourself as their equal. Do not patronise children or be condescending.
- Your interview technique must be relevant to the child's age. There is no point sitting down at a table with a four year old and asking them lots of questions. You will achieve nothing. Play is a wonderful way to communicate with children: dolls, action figures, drawing – and if you think the family may not have toys to play with, take your own.
- Join in. Play with the child. Do your own drawing, make your own tower. If the child thinks you are engrossed in what you are doing, they will be more relaxed and may feel more able to talk. Keep on doing your drawing if a five year old tells you, 'Daddy put his winkie in my bottom and it was sore.' If you stop and look at the child, they may well sense this is important and clam up. Remember, with an older child who knows they are telling you about abuse, you would take a different approach.
- The car can be the perfect place to talk. Many a time I have taken a circuitous route to our destination – I would never get a job as a cab

driver. It is often easier to talk if we are not being looked at in the eye and for a child a car often feels a safe place to talk.

■ Depending on the child's age, explain why you are there and what the likely outcome is. Children often report that we ask them lots of questions but tell them nothing. They will want to know, and deserve to know, what is going on.

■ You need to be sure you understand what the child is telling you and that you are not making assumptions. For example, I knew a small boy, who at the age of two to three loved playing with sticks and, wherever we were, he would find a stick. The only problem was he could not say 'stick' but instead would say 'dick'. He was always telling anyone who would listen how he loved playing with dicks. It would have been easy to jump to the wrong conclusion. Equally another little girl is currently obsessed with binoculars, however, she calls them 'knockers' and is always asking her mother for her 'knockers'. Beware of making assumptions.

The other point to make about language is that it moves on, and again we can make assumptions about what a young person is saying to us. (I remember telling my nephew about a present I had bought for someone and he kept saying it was 'sick'. I was rather offended and surprised because normally he is very polite and lovely. It was only later on in the conversation I realised that 'sick' meant 'cool'!)

If the child has a learning difficulty, or disability, or the parent does, and this is not your area, speak to professionals with the expertise before you visit. Find out the best way to communicate with that service user. To be effective you need to be prepared.

Point of law

Social workers cannot insist on seeing a child alone, either in the family home or anywhere else.

When we are visiting a family at home, we cannot insist we see the child alone, and our consideration of the benefit of seeing them alone will depend on their age and ability, as well as acknowledgement of the fact that it may be frightening for the child. It is difficult to generalise but if I am meeting a child for the first time and they are under two, I would not presume to see them alone. With a child of three or four, I may well say to the mother that I need to see the child's bedroom and I would really like to speak to the child. I would then ask the child to show me their bedroom. I would only do that when I had been in the home for a little while and had probably been sitting on the floor, playing with a toy with the child while I spoke to the mother.

SEEING A SLEEPING BABY

If we are told when we visit a home that the baby is asleep, and we cannot see them, we need to weigh up the risks. This book is about home visits in child protection cases and I would argue that we cannot come away from a home containing a baby without seeing him or her. It is the under-ones who are the most vulnerable and, if we are to assess the level of risk, we need to see the baby. We need to explain that to the primary carer and it may be that you are satisfied by standing at the bedroom door and seeing the baby is asleep and breathing.

 Reminder: Waking the baby

Only wake a baby in extreme circumstances, unless it is your job to weigh the baby, or examine the baby, as part of the child protection work.

As always, the actions we take are based on our own professional judgement but, if in doubt, we should seek advice from others who have more experience. Remember, we are all learning all the time.

Good practice checklist:
Once in the home

✓ Establish who is in the home at the time of your visit, and ask for names and their relationship to the children.
✓ Ensure that you see the entire house, particularly the children's bedrooms.
✓ Talk to the children using techniques relevant to their age.
✓ Ensure that you see sleeping babies.

Before you leave, make sure all the questions you had written down have been answered and you have all the basic information you require, such as who is living in the home, who has **parental responsibility** and who the child spends time with.

6 What to look out for: using observational skills

CLUES AND IMPRESSIONS FROM THE CHILD

As professionals, we need to know about child development. There are many online resources that will explain child development[1], which examine child development up to the age of five. There are also many books that deal with child development. See 'Further reading and resources' for more suggestions if you feel you would like to refresh your knowledge in this area.

There can only be general rules and there will always be exceptions, but part of our assessment of the child should be how they present physically and emotionally. A young child may well be wary of a stranger and that is a natural response. Most young children look to their primary carer for reassurance, either with a look or by moving closer, while in contrast a child who is neglected may well be much more forward. How often do we experience a three year old who, on our first visit to the family, climbs on our knee and tries to claim our attention – perhaps thrusting a book in our face? It may well be that the child is so desperate for attention that he has lost his natural caution but it may not be; so again do not make an assumption. What other evidence is there that would support the theory that this child is starved of attention?

DISGUISED COMPLIANCE

This is a term first used by Peter Reder, Sylvia Duncan and Moira Gray (1993). The NSPCC defines the term as follows: 'A parent or carer

Example from practice

I was working with a woman who had recently fled from an abusive relationship. She was living with her five children aged between eight months and 12 years. One day I was visiting the family and the baby was in his usual position lying in a pushchair with a bottle. I was at the property for an hour and a quarter, and during my visit children returned from school, uniformed police visited, there were several arguments and lots of tears. Throughout all the commotion, the baby fed himself, fell asleep, dropped the bottle, woke up, found the bottle, fed himself, dropped the bottle, could not find it again and lay there staring at the wall. During that whole time the baby asked nothing of anyone and did not make a noise. He had learned early on that there was no point crying because no one responded. He was also unable to sit unsupported, in this case evidence that, because he spent most of his time strapped in a pushchair, his muscles were not developing as they should.

Remember that if there are concerns about a child's development, there should always be a clinical assessment by a medic.

giving the appearance of co-operating with child welfare agencies to avoid raising suspicions, to allay professional concerns and ultimately to diffuse professional intervention.' We saw this with Peter Connelly's mother, Tracey Connelly. She presented as a mother who was concerned about her son, who took him to the doctor when he had injuries from 'falls'. It is easy to be lulled in to a false sense of security by the parent/carer who ostensibly is caring and doing all that is asked of them. We need to look beyond – what is the evidence that the child's life is improving? (In Peter Connelly's case, his weight plummeted from being on the 75th centile when he was born, to the 9th centile.)

A serious case review, SCRCE00 East Cheshire, in February 2011, concluded that the approach of 'many professionals' was affected by perceptions and assumptions made regarding parents' social class, professional status and high academic qualifications.

> [Professionals were] lulled by the parents' disguised compliance. They presented as being concerned for Child B's welfare – which to an extent they may have been. They usually reported him missing, and often made efforts themselves to locate him. In addition they were active in supporting the school's efforts to deal with his challenging behaviour and running away from school.

The NSPCC has produced a useful fact sheet on disguised compliance and the links with serious case reviews.[2] What we know is that, to combat it, we have to work closely with other agencies, ideally use chronologies, supervision should be part of the checks and balances along the way to make sure things are really changing and we need to focus on outcomes, not process. There is a lot of talk about working together and how we can do that effectively and where we have been remiss. When people describe what they see as effective working together they often describe the processes – meetings well attended, healthy challenge, information sharing, etc. – but all good working together is, is things getting better for the child. Every time you do a visit, or you are preparing for a visit, ask yourself that question: 'Are things getting better for the child?' If the answer to that is 'no', you need to question what you are achieving.

We need to be clear that part of our assessment will be what we are told by those around the children, but greater weight should be given to the evidence. Is the situation improving for the child?

As always, we need to be open and honest with the families we are working with – tell a parent if you believe they are trying to deceive or manipulate you, and explain your reasons. Do not be confrontational but present them with the evidence. For example: 'I know you have made it very clear that you support the therapeutic work that the Child and Adolescent Mental Health Service is doing with your child, but actually X has missed four appointments because you have said you have been unable to get him there and you have not attended the two appointments you have been offered. I would like to talk about why that is.'

✓ **Good practice point: Sharing information**

I was working with a mother who had two children, both of whom were subject to child protection plans because of concerns about neglect. One of the children had a serious skin condition that needed careful and constant management. As part of the plan, it was agreed that the mother would take the child to the health visitor's clinic once a week, so she could monitor the skin condition and the mother's treatment of it. After a few weeks the mother told me the health visitor had said she needed to go to the clinic only every two weeks, because she was managing the skin condition well. Although I had no evidence at that point, my gut instinct about this mother was that she was devious and manipulative. I contacted the health visitor to verify what the mother had told me. I then found out that the mother had told the health visitor that I had said she needed to go to the clinic only every two weeks because I was no longer concerned about her treatment of the skin condition.

In this case, the health visitor and I agreed we would do a joint visit to the mother. She needed to know that we were working closely together (this is even more important in cases of disguised compliance). We had a discussion with the mother and she came away knowing that, with this issue, she could not pull the wool over our eyes as we were **sharing information**. She continued to be a challenge to work with.

✓ **Good practice point: Holding babies**

As part of observing how children present physically and emotionally, we should be holding babies. It is not suggested that, as soon as you go into a home, you ask to hold the baby, but when you have been there a while, talking to the **primary carer**, while making eye contact with and cooing at the baby, ask the primary carer if you can hold him/her. We can learn a lot from how responsive a baby is, whether the baby looks to his/her primary carer for reassurance, whether the primary carer hands the baby over without a care. You may also be able to tell if the baby has any physical injuries when you hold him/her – there may be a limb that hangs awkwardly, the baby may cry out when you move him/her.

OBSERVING HOW THE CHILD PLAYS

In Chapter 5 we looked at how to communicate with children. In this chapter we are looking at what to observe. While we are talking to others in the home, we should observe the child. Are they playing? Is there anything to play with? How are they playing? There is so much to learn from observing the child in their home environment.

Example from practice

During a home visit I was in deep conversation with the mother. Her eight-year-old son was playing on the floor. He was playing with a child's doctor's kit and I noticed him pick up the plastic syringe and 'inject' himself in his arm, having bent his elbow. His mother was an intravenous drug user. He knew exactly what to do with a syringe.

OBSERVING HOW THE ADULTS AND CHILDREN INTERACT

There is a considerable amount of research that tells us of the importance of a child having a primary carer who is able to prioritise their child's needs above their own. This now forms the basis of attachment theory, which was first defined by John Bowlby in the 1940s and went on to be developed by Mary Ainsworth and others (Bowlby, 1951; Ainsworth, 1968; Ainsworth, Bell and Stayton, 1974). As part of our assessment, it is essential that we ascertain whether the child we are working with has this positive attachment.

Good practice point: Observing the adults and children together

- ■ Watch how the adults in the home respond to the child – do they respond?
- ■ Does the primary carer respond to the baby's cry, or is he/she absorbed in telling you his/her own problems?
- ■ Does the primary carer just put the dummy back in the baby's mouth, without making eye contact, and continue talking about her/himself?
- ■ Does the primary carer stop to pick up the baby and soothe him/her?
- ■ Does the baby demand anything of the primary carer?
- ■ Does the child look to the mother for reassurance (this is a natural response in a young child) or does the child come straight to you and ignore the mother?
- ■ Does the primary carer answer all the questions you put to the child?
- ■ Does the child appear fearful, or watchful?
- ■ Is the primary carer controlling the interview?
- ■ Does the child flinch when the primary carer moves quickly?
- ■ How would you describe the atmosphere in the room?

Example from practice

I was visiting the home of a family where there were concerns about physical abuse of the children. The father was present and during the meeting he walked quickly to where his three-year-old son was sitting on the floor. The father was not angry but, as he approached his son, the boy cowered and covered his head with his arms. That action gave a very clear picture of what that child's experience with his father was.

We can also learn a lot from how a child responds to their primary carer becoming upset or angry. Does the child register emotion, or do they appear to be oblivious to the tears, the raised voice? I heard of a mother recently who became very upset and her three-year-old son said to her, 'Have your pills, mummy, and you will feel better.' In his world, that was what you did if you were sad.

 Reminder: Cultural differences

Child protection is an area where we need to pay particular heed to cultural differences. It is easy to make an assumption that the black African mother who does not play with her child does not have a strong bond with her child. We need to find out more. Maybe she comes from a tribe where the children play together and the mothers do not have time to play because they have to collect the water, find the firewood, cook the food and wash the clothes in the river, among other things. Even understanding that, it may remain a concern because that mother is no longer living with her tribe but lives in isolation in a tower block and the child has no input from anyone.

However, if we understand why there is so little communication between the mother and the child, at least we can think about what support we can offer that mother, in the alien environment she is living in.

OBSERVING HOW THE ADULTS IN THE HOME PRESENT

There are many factors that affect how children are treated by their families. As stated previously, there is a strong link between parents and carers being perpetrators or victims of domestic abuse, suffering from mental ill-health and/or abusing substances, and the children in those families being abused and/or neglected. The risk to the child increases exponentially if more than one of those factors is in place.

 Reminder: Parent with mental illness

It is important to stress that just because a parent has a diagnosed, or undiagnosed, mental illness, this does not automatically mean that their child will be being abused and/or neglected. It depends entirely on what the illness is and whether the parent/carer is willing or able to accept they have an illness.

Here are two contrasting examples.

Example from practice 1

A mother I worked with had been diagnosed as suffering from bipolar disorder. She had a very good understanding of her illness and was willing to accept she had a mental illness. She shared the care of her children with her mother because she could not manage all the time on her own, but she was a devoted mother. She would say to the professionals, 'You will know when I am going downhill because I will stop wearing make-up and I will smell.' She usually wore a lot of make-up and personal hygiene was not an issue. Sure enough, I would visit one day and she would look a bit rough. I would visit the next day and she would look terrible. I would then contact her community psychiatric nurse. She had periods where she was very unwell and had to be hospitalised. During those times the arrangement she had made with her mother was that her mother would care for the children full-time. On her return home she always needed some time to paint the flat – during her manic phases she would paint the flat in psychedelic colours – and, once she had restored order, she was as capable and as loving as any other mother, always putting her children's needs before her own.

Example from practice 2

I worked with another mother who was completely unable or unwilling to accept that she suffered from mental ill-health. Her illness rendered her incapable of caring for her children. She had periods where she would not sleep for several days at a time but would remain awake and talk constantly, regardless of whether anyone was in the room. She would become paranoid about ghosts and aliens taking over her home, and forget she had children. Sometimes she saw her children as the threat. The Court removed her children because she was unable to care for them. Perhaps if she had been willing to have a mental health assessment, her illness might have been treated and she might have been able to care for her children. Sadly, we will never know.

It is vital that we guard against feeling so much compassion for the adult victim of domestic abuse, the mother who is an intravenous drug user, who was sexually abused as a child, the mother who is a victim of domestic abuse and now abuses alcohol to blot out the terror of her daily life, that we forget why we are there. We are there because there are concerns that a child is being neglected and/or abused, and it is the child who must remain the focus of our visit and the focus of our work and our assessments.

Good practice point: Observing how the animals in the home present

There are strong links between the abuse of animals and the abuse of women and children. If there is an emaciated dog that snarls and shakes, we need to think why that might be and ask questions.

OBSERVING THE STATE OF THE HOME

We have already considered this question in terms of general conditions in Chapter 5. What I want you to do now is consider it in the context of any issues there may be in the home. I have been in more homes than I can number where there have been punch holes in the doors and dents in the walls, and yet the family assures me there are no issues of violence. Do we all have punch marks in our walls?

Good practice point: Maintain your position in court

I was involved in a court case where the father wanted unsupervised contact with his newborn baby. He had been assessed by an 'expert' whose conclusion was that this man was no longer using cannabis habitually and no longer drank alcohol to excess – this conclusion was based on self-reporting by the father. In court, his barrister argued that, as he did not have 'issues with his anger', he should be allowed unsupervised contact with his baby. (He was not living with the mother of the baby.) When I was cross-examined by his barrister, I told the court that I disagreed with the conclusion. There really was an audible gasp in the courtroom that I, a lowly social worker, had dared to disagree with an eminent psychologist, who was an expert. What the psychologist had not done, but I had, was to spend time in this man's home, with his mother, with whom he lived. I had seen the punch marks in the doors. I had seen the doors broken off their hinges and I had heard her fear about his anger. He did not deny to me that he spent most of each day and night in his bedroom, playing violent computer games and smoking cannabis, and had done so for many years. He had no job and no friends, his world was his room and, when he ventured out, his mother was fearful of his rages.

I had the evidence because of those home visits. The psychologist had his word.

The court did not allow him unsupervised contact and contact was not allowed to take place at his home, which was what he had wanted, but at a Children's Centre.

Sometimes thinking is unclear because many professionals are very conscious of the fact that the family is really struggling to manage financially and 'Who am I to judge them for not having X, when

I can afford what I need.' The answer to this is simple. The questions must always be 'What is the impact on the child's life?' and 'What are the parents spending their money on? Are they prioritising what their child needs?' If the answer to the third question is no, you have to start analysing the situation more. It is important to remember that, although there is a strong correlation between poverty and neglect, poverty does not equal neglect. There are many children there will never be concerns about because the parents are prioritising what their child needs. It might be that the parent eats one meal a day but the child is warm, fed and sheltered.

If there are concerns about neglect of the child you need to consider what is in the home. If the concerns are that it is the middle of winter and the three siblings do not have coats and they have holes in their shoes but the home is full of the latest technology, that needs to be questioned.

The state of the home will tell you so much about how things are for the family. You need to be considering the state of the home and asking yourself the question 'What is the impact on the child?' A few crumbs and dog hair on the carpet are not going to kill anyone, but a hypodermic needle might.

Lord Laming coined the phrase 'healthy scepticism' in the Victoria Climbié inquiry[3] and it is a frequent finding from serious case reviews. In the child protection arena we need to question, question, question, and accept only with evidence and cross-referencing with other agencies.

Everything in this chapter emphasises the importance of our observational skills and using those to back up the evidence we have. In Chapter 5, I warned of assuming the chaotic household will have neglected children in it. The most important factor of a child's life is to have one person who gives unconditionally of themselves. It might be that their mother cannot keep on top of the washing, the washing-up, the cleaning, but if she loves her child, can put her child's needs before her own and meet her child's needs, that is what counts the most. In an ideal world we, as parents, would do it all. Sometimes that is not possible. It is up to us as professionals to remember what is important and what really matters to that child. Just as a primary carer must prioritise their child, so must we as professionals be clear about and prioritise what matters most.

> **Good practice checklist: Using your observational skills**
>
> ✓ Beware of 'disguised compliance' – never assume that what you are being told by a parent or carer is the truth.
> ✓ Always hold babies to assess their relationship with the primary carer.
> ✓ Observe how the adults and children respond to one another.
> ✓ Observe how the child plays.
> ✓ Look out for anything unusual in the physical appearance of the home, e.g. punch holes in walls.

You will also need to effectively record everything that happens on a home visit. I would advise against writing copious notes while you are in the home, but if you are being told about something specific then I would say to the service user, 'If you don't mind, I'm going to write this down now because then I can make sure I get it right with you here'.

Once you have left the home, if you jot the key words down so you do not forget them, when you are back in the office those words will remind you what you need to record. Be very clear about what is fact and what is opinion and, remember, never use the words 'appropriate', 'inappropriate', 'bond' or 'attachment'!

Home visiting is only one part of child protection work, but it is an essential part and I hope that this book has given you some new ideas and will help you in the vital work you all do.

Glossary

This glossary not only explains terms used in this book, it also covers some of the common denominators there are in child protection and the impact of these on our visits to families. Glossary words are given in bold on their first occurrence in the text.

The glossary also explains terminology.

TERMINOLOGY

What is the difference between 'safeguarding children' and 'child protection'?

Many professionals use the words interchangeably, as if they mean the same thing. They do not. The government describes safeguarding as follows: 'Safeguarding is a term which is broader than "child protection" and relates to the action that is taken to promote the welfare of children and protect them from harm. Safeguarding is defined in *Working Together to Safeguard Children* (Department for Education, 2015) as:

- protecting children from maltreatment
- preventing impairment of children's health and development
- ensuring that children grow up in circumstances consistent with the provision of safe and effective care, and
- taking action to enable all children to have the best outcomes.'[1]

What does 'child protection' mean?

The Children Act 1989 introduced the concept of significant harm as the threshold that justifies compulsory intervention in family life in the best interest of children. The local authority has a statutory duty to make enquiries where it has reasonable cause to suspect a child is suffering, or is likely to suffer, significant harm (Section 47), and is therefore a child that is need of protection.

DEFINITIONS

Abuse See *Emotional abuse*, *Physical abuse*, *Sexual abuse*.

Child protection conference Professionals will decide that there needs to be a child protection conference. A child protection conference brings together all the professionals working with the family and the family itself. Reports by the professionals will be submitted to the conference and then those attending the conference will give their professional views as to what the concerns and positives are. If the decision of the professionals at the conference is that the child should be made subject to a *child protection plan*, they will then have to agree which categories of abuse the child is at risk of. The child protection plan will be drawn up with the family and worked on by the *core group*, who will have been identified at the conference.

Child protection plan We used to talk about children on the 'At Risk Register' or the 'Child Protection Register', we now talk about children who are subject to or on a 'child protection plan'. In order for a child to be subject to a child protection plan, there will have been a *child protection conference*. It will have been decided by the professionals at the conference that the child should be made the subject of a child protection plan and the categories of abuse will have been agreed. The conference will meet again, initially after three months, and then every six months, to decide whether the child needs to remain subject to a plan and whether anything else needs to be considered. In the meantime the key professionals and family members, known as the core group, will be meeting regularly to make sure the plan is effective in keeping the child safe and everyone is doing as they should. It is important to remember it is how the professionals work together, and how the family works with the professionals, that keeps the child safe, not 'the plan'.

When there is a child protection plan in place, it is where there is a high level of concern but the child is still thought to be safe in the home. (Some local authorities place children on *interim care orders* at home but this is not common.)

Common themes in child protection work

For many years the UK government commissioned the analysis of the data that came from serious case reviews and the research was then published. This research enabled us to see common themes, three of which are most prevalent and therefore significant: domestic abuse, mental ill-health and substance misuse. This research stopped in 2011, but the government has recently announced that it will start to fund the research again.

Although we must always keep our focus on the child, that does not mean we should see a child in isolation. We must consider what life is like for that child and what their perception of their world is. It is the adults around the child that will have the greatest impact on the child, from the time it is born until it moves out into the wider world. What the research shows us is that, in a significant number of cases, there are substance misuse, mental ill-health or domestic abuse issues with the adults with whom the abused/neglected child is living, and that the risk to the child increases exponentially if more than one of these factors is involved.

Before we visit a family, we should have as much information as possible about that family and any factors that are relevant, first and foremost to the child but also to us, when we visit. For example, if you are visiting a family and you know the mother has a diagnosis of bipolar disorder, you need to understand what that means and how that may impact on your visit.

Core group

When it is decided at a *child protection conference* that the child needs to be made the subject of a *child protection plan*, the core group will be identified by the conference. It will consist of the key professionals involved with the family and the key family members. The core group will work on the child protection plan and will meet ten days after the initial child protection conference and then monthly until the next conference. It is their responsibility to monitor and implement the child protection plan and ensure the child remains safe within the home.

Emergency protection order, s.44 Children Act 1989

The local authority can apply to the Court for an emergency protection order. This gives the local authority the power to remove the children from the family. The order lasts for eight days and can be extended for a further seven.

Emotional abuse

'Emotional abuse is the persistent emotional maltreatment of a child such as to cause severe and persistent adverse effects on the child's emotional development.

'It may involve conveying to children that they are worthless or unloved, inadequate or valued only in so far as they meet the needs of another person. It may include not giving the child opportunities to express their views, deliberately silencing them or "making fun" of what they say or how they communicate.

'It may feature developmentally inappropriate expectations being imposed on children. These may include interactions that are beyond the child's developmental capability, as well as overprotection and limitation of exploration and learning, or preventing the child participating in normal social interaction.

'It may involve seeing or hearing the ill treatment of another. It may involve serious bullying (including cyber bullying), causing children frequently to feel frightened or in danger, or the exploitation or corruption of children.

'Some level of emotional abuse is involved in all types of maltreatment of a child, though it may occur on its own.'

Working Together to Safeguard Children
(Department for Education, 2015)

Interim care order, s.38 Children Act 1989

An interim care order lasts for eight weeks, initially. It may be granted to a local authority when it applies for a care order for a child, while assessments are carried out and long-term plans for the child decided. When there is an interim care order in place, the local authority has shared parental responsibility for the child named in the order.

Neglect

'Neglect is the persistent failure to meet a child's basic physical and/or psychological needs, likely to result in the serious impairment of the child's health or development. Neglect may occur during pregnancy as a result of maternal substance abuse. Once a child is born, neglect may involve a parent or carer failing to do the following:

- Provide adequate food, clothing and shelter (including exclusion from home or abandonment).
- Protect a child from physical and emotional harm or danger.
- Ensure adequate supervision (including the use of inadequate care-givers).
- Ensure access to appropriate medical care or treatment.
- Neglect of, or unresponsiveness to, a child's basic emotional needs.'

Working Together to Safeguard Children
(Department for Education, 2015)

Parental responsibility

Parental responsibility is defined by the Children Act 1989 as 'all the rights, duties, powers, responsibilities and authority which by law a parent of a child has in relation to the child and his property'. Therefore, if you have parental responsibility, you have all the legal powers to make appropriate decisions in relation to the upbringing of your child. When there is an emergency protection order, *interim care order* or care order in place, the local authority 'shares' parental responsibility with the parents. I put the word 'share' in inverted commas here because I believe it is an unhelpful euphemism. The local authority has greater power than the parents, if any of the above orders are in place.

As a parent with parental responsibility, you will never lose parental responsibility unless your child is adopted.

Physical abuse	'Physical abuse may involve hitting, shaking, throwing, poisoning, burning or scalding, drowning, suffocating, or otherwise causing physical harm to a child. Physical harm may also be caused when a parent or carer fabricates the symptoms of, or deliberately induces, illness in a child.' *Working Together to Safeguard Children* (Department for Education, 2015) It now constitutes physical abuse if a child is assaulted and it leaves a mark, or causes mental cruelty (Children Act 2004).
Pre-birth child protection conference	If professionals consider an unborn baby to be at risk of significant harm, it may be decided to convene a pre-birth child protection conference. This will ensure there is a plan in place for when the child is born.
Primary carer	The primary carer may be a parent, grandparent, foster carer or someone else. The primary carer is the one who provides the majority of the day-to-day care of the child.
s.17 of the Children Act 1989	When *social care* is working with a family, they will be doing so either under s.47 of the Children Act 1989, or s.17. The definition of s.47 is set out below, i.e. a child in need of protection. s.17 of the Act refers to children who are 'failing to thrive'. If that is the case, the local authority has a responsibility to provide services where the health and development of children are being avoidably impaired. Children who come under s.17 are often defined as 'children in need'. s.17 is where there is a lower level of concern.
s.47 of the Children Act 1989	The local authority has a statutory duty to make enquiries where it has reasonable cause to suspect a child is suffering, or is likely to suffer significant harm. This is s.47 of the Children Act 1989. In other words, s.47 is when it is believed a child is being abused or neglected.
Serious case reviews	As set out in *Working Together to Safeguard Children* (Department for Education, 2015), a serious case review

will always take place whenever a child dies and there is thought to be an aspect of abuse or neglect. There may also be a serious case review when a child has suffered serious injury through abuse or neglect, when a child has been seriously harmed as a result of being sexually abused, when a parent has been murdered and a domestic homicide review is initiated, or a child has been seriously injured following a violent assault by another child or an adult *and* there are concerns about how individuals and/or agencies have worked together.

The Local Safeguarding Children Board (LSCB) is responsible for conducting the serious case review.

The main purpose of a serious case review is to examine what has happened and to try to learn lessons, to improve practice.

Service user

Again, different professionals have different terms for their clients, and different words go in and out of fashion. Currently social care talk about 'service users', meaning the families they are working with, and that is the term used in this book.

Sexual abuse

'Sexual abuse involves forcing or enticing a child or young person to take part in sexual activities, not necessarily involving a high level of violence, whether or not the child is aware of what is happening.

'The activities may involve physical contact, including assault by penetration (e.g. rape or oral sex) or non-penetrative acts such as masturbation, kissing, rubbing and touching outside of clothing. They may include noncontact activities, such as involving children in looking at, or in the production of, sexual images, watching sexual activities, encouraging children to behave in sexually inappropriate ways, or grooming a child in preparation for abuse (including via the internet). Sexual abuse is not solely perpetrated by adult males. Women can also commit acts of sexual abuse, as can other children.'

Working Together to Safeguard Children
(Department for Education, 2015)

Sharing information

There is much confusion about when and whether to share information about families. Best practice would say that we would have the family's permission to share information with other agencies, however, in terms of child protection, it is not a requirement. Legally we talk about sharing information if it is in the 'public interest', and what that means for us working in child protection is where there is a clear likelihood that a child is suffering, or is likely to suffer, significant harm, agencies should be sharing relevant information, regardless of whether they have the family's permission to do so. Child protection overrides data protection and the human rights of the adults.

If social care is working under s.47 of the Children Act 1989, permission does not have to be sought, or given. If we are working under s.17, we cannot share information without parental consent.

One of the common themes arising from serious case reviews is that agencies are not good at sharing information and information tends to be shared when it is too late, when the child has died. Unfortunately, we will never reach the point where we will be able to prevent every child from dying from abuse or neglect, but there is no doubt we would do a better job at protecting children if we shared information before it is too late.

All you have to remember is: all agencies have to share information if they are undertaking a child protection investigation, or working with a child under s.47 of the Children Act 1989.

Significant harm

The Children Act 1989 introduced the concept of significant harm as 'The threshold which justifies compulsory intervention in family life in the best interest of children. The Local Authority has a statutory duty to make enquiries where it has reasonable cause to suspect a child is suffering, or is likely to suffer significant harm' (Section 47).

Social care

For the purpose of this book 'social care' refers to those working in the social work departments of local authorities. It is confusing that, to different professionals, the term has different meanings. To the government, 'social care' appears to refer only to adult services, whereas those of us working in children's services refer to ourselves working in 'social care'. The term 'social services' is also still used by some.

Strategy discussion

As set out in *Working Together to Safeguard Children* (Department for Education, 2015), when a referral is made to *social care*, if it is thought to be a child protection case, the local authority's social care department has a duty to hold a strategy discussion involving police, health, social care and 'other bodies as appropriate, in particular the referring agency'. The purpose of the discussion is to decide on the next course of action.

Notes

1 SETTING THE SCENE

1 www.gov.uk/government/uploads/system/uploads/attachment_data/file/273183/5730.pdf
2 http://dera.ioe.ac.uk/723/1/second%20serious%20case%20overview%20report%20relating%20to%20peter%20connelly%20dated%20march%202009.pdf
3 www.bradford-scb.org.uk/scr/hamzah_khan_scr/Serious%20Case%20Reveiw%20Overview%20Report%20November%202013.pdf
4 www.lscbbirmingham.org.uk/images/stories/downloads/executive-summaries/Case_25__Final_Overview_Report_02.10.13.pdf
5 www.gov.uk/government/uploads/system/uploads/attachment_data/file/181651/DFE-RR040.pdf
6 www.rotherham.gov.uk/downloads/file/1407/independent_inquiry_cse_in_rotherham

2 PREPARING FOR THE VISIT

1 http://dera.ioe.ac.uk/723/1/second%20serious%20case%20overview%20report%20relating%20to%20peter%20connelly%20dated%20march%202009.pdf

3 KEEPING YOURSELF SAFE

1 www.hse.gov.uk/violence/toolkit/examplepolicy.pdf
2 www.workingtogetheronline.co.uk/documents/learning_lessons_from_serious_case_reviews_20092010.pdf

4 GETTING IN THE DOOR

1 www.bradford-scb.org.uk/scr/hamzah_khan_scr/Serious%20Case%20Reveiw%20Overview%20Report%20November%202013.pdf

5 ONCE IN THE HOME

1 www.coventrylscb.org.uk/files/SCR/FINAL%20Overview%20Report%20%20DP%20130913%20Publication%20version.pdf
2 www.gov.uk/government/uploads/system/uploads/attachment_data/file/273183/5730.pdf

6 WHAT TO LOOK OUT FOR: USING OBSERVATIONAL SKILLS

1 www.nhs.uk/Tools/Pages/birthtofive.aspx#close and http://webarchive.nationalarchives.gov.uk/20130401151715/http://www.education.gov.uk/publications/eOrderingDownload/eyfs_cards_0001207.pdf
2 www.nspcc.org.uk/globalassets/documents/information-service/case-reviews-disguised-compliance.pdf
3 www.gov.uk/government/uploads/system/uploads/attachment_data/file/273183/5730.pdf

GLOSSARY

1 www.gov.uk/government/publications/safeguarding-children-and-young-people/safeguarding-children-and-young-people

Further reading and resources

The list of further reading and resources below is designed to provide a range of signposts to expand your knowledge base across the various areas considered. This is divided into different areas to help you to quickly identify the information you need.

KEEPING YOURSELF UP TO DATE

One of the key elements that you need to consider in child protection is the maintenance of your own knowledge and skills. As a social worker you are expected to have a detailed knowledge of your area, and the evidence that supports different interventions and outcomes. This knowledge can be difficult to maintain up to date in rapidly changing services and structures, so it is important that you consider how you are going to sustain your competence and ensure that your practice is evidence based. Books, magazines, journals and research reports are widely available, and you will need to consider which formats you prefer to use to access information.

The internet is a valuable resource for social workers as it offers instant access to a diverse range of information and contacts. Many written publications are also available, and regular press can also help you to maintain your knowledge base and ensure your recommendations are based on the most up-to-date evidence available.

These resources will help to get you started when you are newly qualified, and help you to both improve your practice and to keep yourself abreast of developments across the social work profession as you continue your career.

The following resources are organisations/publications that will help to keep you informed. They include a range of information that will provide the foundation of more detailed reading where necessary.

Reminder: Maintaining your knowledge

- Are you aware of the professional journals and press available in your practice area?
- Does your organisation subscribe to any press that you could access?
- Do you have access to Athens (online resources) via your organisation?
- Do you know how to perform a basic internet search for news in your practice area? If not, who could help you with this?
- Do you keep up to date with current affairs in social care? If not, how could you change this?
- Do you subscribe to any newsletters, discussion forums or other professional networking activities? If not, what would be helpful to keep you up to date?
- Do you use supervision to reflect on your practice and development needs? Do you include communication skills in these reflections?

RESOURCES

- Specific forums for children's social work practice can be found on CareSpace: www.communitycare.co.uk/carespace/forums/default. aspx
- *Children and Young People Now* is a magazine you can access online. It also makes available all the latest news, research and

best practice for those working in social care and other related professions. Access is limited unless a fee is paid: www.cypnow.co.uk
- *Community Care* is the online trade magazine for social care practitioners. It includes articles, research updates, practice forums and links to discussion forums for social workers on many different issues: www.communitycare.co.uk
- Does your organisation subscribe to *Community Care Inform*? It is an online comprehensive data source that contains a wealth of expert-written, practice-related information, including guidance to key pieces of legislation, expert articles and practice guides.
- Social Care Online is a searchable database of social care publications, knowledge and research reviews provided by the Social Care Institute for Excellence (SCIE). They describe themselves as having the 'UK's most complete range of information and research on all aspects of social care': www.scie-socialcareonline.org.uk

A number of organisations publish research and practice in this field, including the NSPCC (www.nspcc.org.uk) and Ofsted (www.ofsted.gov.uk).

Other sites that will be useful for all types of practice include those listed below.

- NSPCC professionals website: www.nspcc.org.uk/Inform/informhub_wda49931.html. Includes a range of information and news concerning safeguarding children, as well as resources and research information.
- www.actionforchildren.org.uk
- Research into serious case reviews is published by the Department for Education and can be found on its website: www.education.gov.uk. Ofsted also publishes serious case review data.
- The report of the Munro Review of Child Protection (Munro, 2011) includes some key findings and practice implications: www.education.gov.uk/publications/standard/Childrenandfamilies/Page1/CM%208062

LEGISLATION AND STATUTORY GUIDELINES

Most of the legislation and statutory guidelines that you are likely to need are available on the internet. Listed below are the key websites that will provide you with a comprehensive range of documents and resources to inform your practice.

- The Department for Education website (www.education.gov.uk) publishes a range of policy, practice guidance, statutory guidance and government papers regarding children, young people and education.
- Legislation Online (www.legislation.gov.uk) publishes Acts of Parliament, statutory instruments and ministerial orders across the UK.
- Your employer will have policies and procedures on employee safety and lone working – however, for the national perspective and legislation, details can be found through the Health and Safety Executive: www.hse.gov.uk

PROFESSIONAL STANDARDS

Social work is carried out in accordance with codes of practice and these should underpin all your practice activities.

Social workers are regulated by the Health & Care Professions Council (www.hpc-uk.org). All social workers should be aware of its standards for professional training, professional skills, behaviour and health.

FURTHER READING

Baron-Cohen, S. (2011) *Zero Degrees of Empathy: A New Theory of Human Cruelty*. London: Allen Lane.
Batmanghelidjh, C. (2007) *Shattered Lives: Children Who Live with Courage and Dignity*. London: Jessica Kingsley Publishers.

Corby, B., Shemmings, D. and Wilkins, D. (2012) *Child Abuse: An Evidence Base for Confident Practice*, 4th edn. Maidenhead: Open University Press.

Howe, D. (2005) *Child Abuse and Neglect: Attachment, Development and Intervention*. Basingstoke: Palgrave Macmillan.

Parrish, M. (2014) *Social Work Perspectives on Human Behaviour*, 2nd edn. Maidenhead: Open University Press.

Shemmings, D. and Shemmings, Y. (2014) *Assessing Disorganised Attachment Behaviour in Children*. London: Jessica Kingsley Publishers.

Ward, H., Brown, R., Westlake, D. and Davies, C. (2012) *Safeguarding Babies and Very Young Children from Abuse and Neglect (Safeguarding Children Across Services)*. London: Jessica Kingsley Publishers.

References

Ainsworth, M.D.S. (1968) Object relations, dependency, and attachment: a theoretical review of the infant–mother relationship. *Child Development*, 40: 969–1025.

Ainsworth, M.D.S., Bell, S.M. and Stayton, D. (1974) Infant–mother attachment and social development. In M.P. Richards (ed.) *The Introduction of the Child into a Social World*. Cambridge: Cambridge University Press, pp. 99–135.

Bowlby, J. (1951) *Maternal Care and Mental Health*. Geneva: World Health Organization.

Braithwaite, R. (n.d.) *Guide to How to Deal with Hostile and Aggressive Adults or Young People and How to Manage Intimidating Situations*. Available online at: www.ccinform.co.uk

Brandon, M., Bailey, S. and Belderson, P. (2009) *Serious Case Reviews: A Two-year Analysis of Child Protection Database Notifications 2007–2009*. Research Report DFE-RR040. London: DfE.

Department for Education (2013) *Working Together to Safeguard Children: A Guide to Inter-agency Working to Safeguard and Promote the Welfare of Children*. London: DfE.

Ferguson, H. (2009) Performing child protection: home visiting, movement and the struggle to reach the abused child. *Child and Family Social Work*, 14(4): 471–80.

London Borough of Brent (1985) *A Child in Trust: Report of the Panel of Inquiry into the Circumstances Surrounding the Death of Jasmine Beckford*. London: Borough of Brent.

Munro, E. (2010) *The Munro Review of Child Protection Part One: A Systems Analysis*. London: DfE.

Munro, E. (2011) *The Munro Review of Child Protection: Final Report: A Child-centred System*. Available online at: www.education.gov.uk/publications/standard/Childrenandfamilies/Page1/CM%208062

Reder, P., Duncan, S. and Gray, M. (1993) *Beyond Blame: Child Abuse Tragedies Revisited*. London: Routledge.

Index

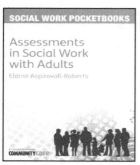

ASSESSMENTS IN SOCIAL WORK WITH ADULTS

Elaine Aspinwall-Roberts

9780335245215 (Paperback)
May 2012

eBook also available

This accessible survival guide shows social workers how to make their assessments the best, most effective and person-centred they can be.

Part of a new Social Work Pocketbooks series, the book is friendly, non-patronising and realistic about the day-to-day difficulties and challenges associated with assessing adults. It encourages you to reflect on how you work, and what you bring to the task.

Key features:

- Practical examples, advice and tips, including dealing with pitfalls
- Good practice and point of law reminders
- Fresh ideas on how to develop your assessment skills with adults

www.openup.co.uk

OPEN UNIVERSITY PRESS
McGraw - Hill Education

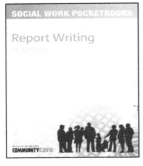

REPORT WRITING

Daisy Bogg

9780335245130 (Paperback)
May 2012

eBook also available

Report writing is a key social work skill, and one in which many practitioners receive very little formal training and preparation.

Part of a new Social Work Pocketbooks series published in association with Community Care, this easy to use guide will assist you in producing professional, informative and good quality reports. It provides key information, hints and tips to help you to develop your report writing style and to consider best practice in your written communication.

Key features:

- A range of report templates
- Examples of good practice in report writing
- Specialist chapters covering legal, policy and assessment situations

www.openup.co.uk

OPEN UNIVERSITY PRESS
McGraw - Hill Education

Working with Substance Users

Kim Heanue and Chris Lawton

9780335245192 (Paperback)
2012

eBook also available

This book, part of the Pocketbook series, will be a useful tool not only for experienced professionals but also newly qualified social workers and students. It deals with topics such as why people take substances and the risks involved as well as suggesting ways to deal with challenging situations.

Key features:

- A practical desk guide for social workers to refer to on a day-to-day basis.

www.openup.co.uk

OPEN UNIVERSITY PRESS
McGraw - Hill Education